Fiery Cuisines

Fiery Cuisines

Hot and spicy dishes from around the world

Dave DeWitt and Nancy Gerlach

Macdonald

A *Macdonald* BOOK

© American edition
Dave DeWitt and Nancy Gerlach 1984
© English adaptations and illustrations
Macdonald and Co (Publishers) Ltd 1985

First published in Great Britain in 1985
by Macdonald & Co (Publishers) Ltd
London & Sydney

A member of BPCC plc

British Library Cataloguing in Publication Data
DeWitt, Dave
    Fiery cuisines
    1. Cookery (Spices)   2. Spices
    I. Title   II. Gerlach, Nancy
    641.6383   TX819.A1

    ISBN 0-356-10966-6

Designer: Kate Poole
Photographer: Eric Carter
Stylist: Dawn Lane
Home Economist: Roz Denny
Indexer: Michèle Clark

Filmset by Goodfellow & Egan, Cambridge

Printed and bound in Great Britain by
Purnell & Sons (Book Production) Ltd,
Paulton, Bristol
A member of the BPCC Group

Macdonald & Co (Publishers) Ltd
Maxwell House
74 Worship Street
London EC2A 2EN

Contents

Recipe Index

◆ Poultry Dishes

(see Combination Dishes)

◆ Seafood Dishes

SHELLFISH

FISH

◆ Egg and Cheese Dishes

◆ Pasta, Rice and Potatoes

◆ Vegetables

◆ Breads

How it all began

In a cosy restaurant near the harbour in Nassau in the West Indies two young tourists are glancing through the lunch menu. It seems innocuous enough. *Seafood Salad* – sounds good, and when it comes it looks even better – a small bowl of chopped seafood with onion and some sort of fresh green vegetable. The man raises the first modest forkful to his lips and notices a wonderful aroma. Encouraged, he takes a mouthful.

Immediately, a sensation unlike anything he has ever experienced before spreads across his tongue, engulfs his mouth and seems to cauterize his throat. 'Good grief, that's hot!' he exclaims, tears streaming down his face. He is not sure if he should continue eating, but he's fascinated. The salad is terrifically hot, but it tastes fantastic.

His next timid sampling is easier to take; his mouth is either numb or adapting. By the time the bowl is empty, the man is perspiring, but proud. He's done it! He's finished the hottest food he's ever tasted. Little does he know that one bowl of scallops with serrano chillies has changed his life. From that time on his eating habits will never be the same. He's hooked on hot foods.

Scenes such as this are repeated every day as people discover what enthusiasts have known for years – hot and spicy food can be delicious. That discovery has led to an appreciation of fiery foods from all parts of the globe. It is our hope that this cookbook will both introduce newcomers to the delicious world of hot-food cooking and broaden the tastes of those who have come to love spicy dishes and are looking for the best and tastiest recipes.

Everyone knows at least one hot-food lover. These are the people with mouths of asbestos who dare to order the Vindaloo in an Indian restaurant without flinching, who eat the 'extra hot' Szechuan dishes at their favourite Chinese restaurant, and who liberally sprinkle Tabasco sauce on their scrambled eggs in the morning. They have learnt that cooking 'hot' food does not necessarily mean preparing dishes that scorch the tonsils; rather that it is a cuisine that blends heat, fragrance and flavour to produce spicy gourmet delicacies. And there's no doubt about it, the interest in hot foods is spreading.

One of the major reasons for this new enthusiasm is the fact that these dishes are exotic, yet easy to prepare. Our taste buds can travel to Africa for the piquant combination of peanuts and chillies, to central Europe for the combined powers of paprika and horse-radish, and to Sri Lanka for perhaps the hottest curries of all, laced with green chillies, ginger and mustard seeds.

Perhaps the burning sensation in our recipes is not for everyone, but it really is not necessary to make the meals so scorching hot that they cannot possibly be tasted or appreciated. As we shall see, there are many possible heat levels and quite a number of different 'hot' ingredients that combine perfectly to produce fiery yet delicious dishes.

Firepower: where it comes from

Of the four-hundred-odd spices in the world, the most pungent are the most popular. Although only chilli truly scorches, there are a handful of others that approach the firepower of chilli.

Black pepper, horseradish, ginger, mustard and chillies all add excitement – and fire – to our food. All have varying degrees of heat when used alone or in combination with each other and other spices, and at the end of this chapter you'll find a heat scale to help you gauge the relative pungency of each recipe.

Here is a brief 'history of heat'.

Pepper

'Pepper', said Plato, 'is small in quantity and great in virtue.' It was beloved by the Greeks and was the favourite spice of ancient Rome. Peppercorns were the first Oriental spice to reach Europe and were in such demand that they were used as currency for about two thousand years. Pepper soon became an expression of a man's fortune, and the wealthy kept large stores of pepper in their houses as proof of solvency. One way of saying that a man was poor was that he 'lacked pepper'.

Black pepper is *not* related to chilli 'peppers', which were misnamed by Columbus. Black pepper is a type of climbing vine cultivated throughout the East Indies and often reaching a length of over 12 metres/30 feet. The fruit of this vine is the peppercorn, which resembles (but hardly tastes like) a mistletoe berry. The tiny fruits are picked when they are yellowish-red, and then are immersed in boiling water for about ten minutes. This process turns them black, and then the peppercorns are dried in the sun. Some pepper-corns are picked green and sold fresh. The odour of pepper is penetrating and aromatic, while the taste is bitter and spicy hot.

Today pepper is consumed in great quantities and is probably the most commonly used spice throughout the world. It is usually combined with other spices during cooking, although in a few 'classic' recipes, such as Steak aux Trois Poivres (page 30), it is the principal pungent ingredient.

The radish that's really a mustard

There has always been confusion between the 'salad' radish and horseradish, yet the latter is not a radish at all – it is a root crop more closely related to mustard.

In classical times horseradish was prized for its medicinal qualities. The Greek physician

Dioscorides believed it improved eyesight and aided in relieving cramp. Pliny claimed that horseradish dissolved gallstones, though medical science has yet to confirm his findings. The Romans viewed horseradish suspiciously because they thought it promoted belching (and we know how refined Roman banquets were!).

Horseradish is native to central Europe, where it was first collected in the wild, and later cultivated. Because of its pungency, its consumption was originally considered to be beneath noble tastes and suitable only for peasants. But after its culinary properties were properly recognized, it became the principal ingredient in sauces to be served with roast meats (see page 27). Chaucer described its effect with the admonition: 'Woe to the cook whose sauce has no sting.' Horseradish in a concentrated form can indeed bring tears to the eyes.

There has never been much of a world trade in horseradish because it grows easily in temperate zones throughout the world. In fact, in some cool, moist areas it is regarded as a weed. Most commercial horseradish preparations consist of the grated root alone, perhaps combined with vinegar and salt, or a creamy sauce with the root as its pungent ingredient. Its close relative, *wasabi*, or Japanese horseradish, is used to spice up Sashimi and Sushi (page 76).

Taste gingerly

Ginger is considered to be a native of South-east Asia, where it has been used since ancient times. It was transported to the Mediterranean area in about the first century AD, accompanied by rumours about its supposed powers to cure flatulence and colic. Again, the early users of hot spices tended to put medicine before cooking. Because of the high profits possible from trading, ginger also became one of the most popular spices in the world. By the eleventh century ginger was well known in England, especially for use in baking. A few hundred years later the Spanish introduced ginger into the West Indies and Mexico.

Queen Elizabeth I supposedly invented the gingerbread man by insisting that little ginger cakes be fashioned into likenesses of her friends. The English took it to the Americas, and ginger became part of the standard rations for American soldiers during the Revolutionary War. English appreciation of the spice was sharpened when it was realized that it was one of the most important ingredients of the curry sauces of colonial India.

Ginger has a pleasant, slightly biting taste that can shock the system, especially when a piece is stuck to the roof of the mouth! Fresh ginger root is an important ingredient in chutneys, and tender young roots are often candied, or sliced and preserved in syrup.

Ginger roots are now grown all over the world. Jamaica supplies most of the peeled (white) ginger, India is the source of unpeeled ginger, and West Africa also exports dried ginger roots. Fresh, raw ginger is primarily used in cooking and as a spicy complement to seafood dishes. The extracts and powders from ginger are used extensively in baked goods, meat dishes, soft drinks and ice creams. In home cooking, ground ginger flavours scones, cakes, sauces, curry dishes and pickles. In the dried and powdered form it resembles our next hot spice, mustard.

The hot weed

The origins of mustard are lost in prehistory. Some experts believe that early man began its cultivation. But since mustard is so easy to grow, it is entirely possible that 'cultivation' in this case meant merely scattering the seeds about and waiting. Mustard spreads so rapidly that the Hindus consider it a fertility symbol, so mustard probably began its culinary career as a weed.

Mustard seeds have been collected and used medicinally since ancient times. The Greek father of medicine, Hippocrates, first mentioned the efficacy of mustard seeds for treating colds. Since his time hot mustard baths and plasters have been standard medicine for chest colds. It was the Romans who introduced mustard to Britain, and the best was said to come from Tewkesbury.

The most commonly eaten varieties of the hot weed are white mustard, the stronger black mustard, and – most powerful of all – Indian or Chinese mustard. In Europe and the United States mustard is sold in three ways: as seeds, as a dry powder that is mixed with water, and as a paste or wholegrain preparation that can be blended with other spices, wine and vinegar. Its most common application is to spice up meats and salads, and a good example of its use occurs in our recipe for Fondue Bourguignonne (page 31).

The pungency of mustard is similar to that of horseradish, to which it is related. It doesn't burn so much as shock the senses, particularly the nasal passages. Mustard in any form will lose its pungency as a result of oxidation, so it must be kept tightly sealed.

The fiery fruit

Chilli 'peppers' are one of the earliest domesticated crops of the New World, so it is ironic that hot dishes derived from them took so long to be introduced into the United States. Most history books tell us that Christopher Columbus 'discovered' chillies in the West Indies while searching for India, and that he brought back to Europe, according to historian Peter Martyr in 1493, 'peppers more pungent than that from the Caucasus'. Martyr, of course, is comparing chillies to black pepper from the Caucasus. Chillies are actually the fruits (in the botanical sense of a ripened ovary of a flower, containing seeds) of plants of the *Solanaceae* family, which includes tomatoes and aubergines.

Chillies were first domesticated in Mexico in about 7000 BC. There is little doubt that Columbus *was* the first person to introduce the fiery fruit to Europeans, but tradition holds that Spanish explorers reintroduced chillies to Mexico and the American Southwest during their conquests. This theory has been accepted for decades and suggests that Europeans were more appreciative of hot foods than the primitive societies they were conquering. However, there are many pre-Columbian chilli recipes (page 102), and there is no evidence that the Spanish gave chillies to the Indians; it is much more likely that the Pueblo Indians acquired them through trade with the Toltecs of Mexico.

By 1650 the cultivation and gastronomic use of chillies had spread throughout Europe, Asia and Africa, and the fiery fruits had been adopted into the cuisines of many countries of the world. As befitting their origin, they became most popular in tropical climates. Only the milder forms, like pimentos and paprika, were used in Europe, where the pungency in foods generally came from mustard, horseradish or black pepper.

Outside North and South America the hottest chillies have been cultivated in China, Africa and South-east Asia. Our collection of recipes from those areas illustrates the spread of chillies and the diversity of chilli cuisines around the world.

As the appreciation of hot foods gained popularity in the western United States, the demand for chillies grew so large that imports from Mexico were insufficient. Following the Mexican war of 1848, seeds from a fiery chilli grown in the state of Tabasco were imported to Louisiana and grown by a judge named Avery and a banker named McIlhenny. It was their dream to create a sauce from the Tabasco chilli that could be served with meats, soups and seafood. Thus came the invention of Tabasco sauce, which has been produced and widely exported to become one of the great success stories in chilli lore. Their secret was mashing the Tabasco chillies to a fine paste, aging this paste in oaken casks for three years, then mixing it with vinegar before bottling. Today there are a number of similar sauces on the market.

Although Tabasco sauce has catered for much of our craving for hot spices, cultivation of other varieties of chilli began about 1898 in New Mexico. Today more than fifty thousand tonnes of chillies of many kinds are harvested each year in the United States alone, though India is now thought to be the largest producer.

Chilli heat

Regardless of the form they take – whole, powdered, in oil or sauces – chillies range in heat from spicy-hot to truly inedible. This range is dependent upon the amount of a chemical called *capsicin*, which occurs in veins near the seeds of the chilli. An alkaloid, capsicin is incredibly powerful and stable. The pure form can be detected by human taste buds in a dilution of one part in *one million*. It is seemingly unaffected by cold or heat, retaining its original potency despite time, cooking or freezing. Since it resists oxidation, its power is not diminished by air, as is that of mustard. The degree of heat found in various kinds of chillies is controlled, not by the physical size of the chilli itself, but by genes that modify the amount of capsicin present. Often, the smaller the chilli, the hotter it is. And colour is not always a guide.

We know that chillies are hot, but do they heat you up? Should Eskimos be eating Chile con Carne? And why on earth do sane, normal people eat hot foods in hot weather? Well, the startling fact is that the consumption of chillies makes you *cooler*! The capsicin they contain dilates the blood vessels, which increases blood circulation, thus enabling the body to perspire more. This action throws off heat, since perspiration is the body's natural cooling system.

Because of the fiery nature of chilli pods and powder, it is a good idea to wear gloves while handling chillies. When transferred to the eyes or other sensitive body areas, capsicin can cause severe burning. If you should accidentally be burned, immediately flush the eyes with plenty of fresh water and wash other areas with large amounts of soapy water.

There is a myth that suggests that one becomes 'macho' in direct proportion to the degree of chilli heat one can consume. Some people indulge in jalapeño-eating contests, risking stomach injuries to prove their pungency prowess. Actually, the ability to withstand capsicin is not related to gender or hormones; it is simply a matter of bodily acclimatization. One seems to build up a tolerance to chilli heat gradually, until the tears finally disappear.

A piece of advice: when eating food that is too hot, most people gasp and reach for a glass of water. But capsicin is insoluble in water; like oil and water, they don't mix. Mineral waters and water-based liquids such as beer actually force the capsicin in your stomach, displacing it but not neutralizing it. Dairy products, on the other hand, do neutralize capsicin to a certain degree. So reach for yogurt, soured cream or milk if you've eaten food that is too fiery.

The Scoville Scale

There is some confusion about measuring the relative heat of spicy ingredients because chemical tests do not take into account individual reactions, which differ according to acclimatization. As it turns out, all pungency measurements are subjective. In 1919 an American pharmacologist named Scoville devised a method that is still used today to test for relative heat. A measured weight of chillies is processed to extract the capsicin, and then dilutions are made for testing. A panel of five 'heat experts' is convened for the torture test, and they proceed to taste and evaluate the dilutions. The pungency is recorded in multiples of one hundred 'Scoville units'. A majority of three members of the panel must agree before a rating is assigned and although there is an attempt to be scientific and objective, a Scoville panel resembles a wine-tasting party more than a careful laboratory test. We hope that this collection of recipes will inspire hot food lovers to convene their own Scoville test groups.

On the Scoville scale very mild heat rates about 100 units, while extremely hot chillies score over 10,000 units. We have attempted to construct a pungency rating for each recipe by using the following table. Note that our heat scale is exponential, and thus a rating of eight is not twice as hot as four, but rather *four times* as hot. And please remember that any heat rating is subjective and approximate. *The rating of ten is theoretical and applies only to the very hottest chillies in pure form, not prepared meals.*

Heat scale rating	Hot ingredients	Approximate Scoville units
10	Legendary chilli 'Bahama Mama' and 'Texas Fireball'	20 000+
9	Hontaka (Japanese dried hot chillies)	15 000
8	Tabasco, chilli pequíns, other small hot chillies, Sambals,	12 000
7	Mexican jalapeños, serranos, chilli oil	10 000
6	Some chilli powders	8 000
5	Mexican hot sauces	5 000
4	Pasilla, Fresno, black and dried ancho chillies	3 000
3	Yellow (wax) chillies, curry powder	1 500
2	Black pepper, Chinese mustard	500
1	Ginger, horseradish, other mustards, some small peppers, paprika, pimento	100–200

Note: some American and Mexican chillies are not available outside the United States

How the recipes are organized

The recipes in this book are arranged according to region to show how hot foods are distributed and how they vary throughout the world. With each recipe is a Heat Scale symbol keyed to the table above. We have also included some serving suggestions and variations with as many recipes as possible.

You will be happy to know that the recipes in this book have been selected as much for flavour as for heat. It's easy to increase the heat in any recipe, so the point is not to make dishes that are unbearably hot. The tastiest spicy dishes are those naturally delicious ones that are enhanced by just the right amount of spice to make them truly tasty hot foods. It is important to know the 'firepower' of the ingredients you are using, especially when dealing with chillies or cayenne. Green chillies vary in intensity by variety – often the smaller they are, the hotter. Dried chilli flakes can range from nearly sweet to hot, and the hontaka, or Japanese, dried red chilli should be treated with the greatest respect. As a result a particular recipe can vary from mild to untouchable depending on the quality and the quantity of the fiery ingredients. If in doubt, start with a small amount and taste and add until the desired heat level is reached.

Pungent ingredients

Hot ingredients for use in these recipes should be available in one form or another in many supermarkets. Asian and Chinese grocers are another invaluable source of chillies, chilli preparations and advice. Here is a basic list of what you may expect to find, with some suggestions as to substitutions.

Pepper

There are three basic types of pepper available on the market, which are simply three forms of the same peppercorn. Green peppercorns are picked when fresh, then pickled and bottled. Often they are mashed before being added to a recipe. Dried black peppercorns – the ones we recommend for use in most of our dishes – are used whole, crushed, or powdered. Grinding your own peppercorns as and when you need them gives a fresher, more pungent flavour, and they will keep for months without losing quality. Use ready-ground black pepper if you have to, but the results will not be as strong or tasty. White peppercorns can also be bought. These are the core of the black peppercorn with the outer husk removed, and are most often ground to a powder with some black pepper added for use at table. White pepper is used in recipes, such as those made with fish, where aesthetically black pepper would spoil the look of the dish. Some people avow that white pepper tastes sharper and less pungent. In Chinese shops you will also find Szechuan peppercorns, looking like tiny flower buds.

Horseradish

Fresh horseradish root is available in some shops, or it can be homegrown. It should be peeled and then grated. Don't confuse it with the white radish or mooli, which is paler in colour and more regular in shape. This is much less pungent and is really a salad vegetable. Dried horseradish flakes are a good substitute for the fresh root, as is bottled grated horseradish. If all else fails, use the bottled creamed horseradish, but remember that this is far less pungent, so add more!

Ginger

You can now find fresh ginger root at all times of the year in supermarkets. The characteristic knobbly root should be peeled and sliced or grated, according to the recipe. Ground ginger can be used instead, but lacks that 'extra dimension' of the fresh root. Buy ground ginger in small quantities as and when you need it, though it keeps its pungency for quite a while. The lovely crystallized ginger, and ginger in syrup are obviously best reserved for dessert.

Mustard

The three basic forms of mustard are mustard seeds, dry mustard powder and the prepared proprietary brands, among them English, Dijon (French), and wholegrain varieties. All vary in spiciness, with the black, or Chinese, mustard being the hottest, closely followed by traditional English mustard. Prepared mustards vary quite a lot in flavour – and are worth exploring on their own account – being a combination of dry mustard powder, selected spices, and vinegar. The finest and most pungent are the French mustards from the Dijonnaise region. Prepared mustard may be substituted for mustard powder in most recipes – unless Dijon-style is specified. Your best allies are your taste buds.

Fresh or green chillies

These are appearing with greater frequency in food stores and supermarkets as demand for them grows. It is not easy to gauge the relative heat of the larger chillies, but the standard 'rule' is the larger the chilli, the milder it should be. Fresh red chillies, which are simply the green ones at a later stage of ripeness, are usually less pungent and sweeter in taste – just like green and red peppers. The smaller black-skinned chilli is much hotter, and the longer, thin, tapering, slightly wrinkled red and green chillies are representative of several varieties, all extremely hot. They are sometimes called cayenne chillies, for convenience. Use these when the Mexican jalapeño chilli is specified (the jalapeño itself is a darkish green and about 6 cm/2½ in long). The serrano chilli is slightly milder, shorter – more like a miniature fresh green chilli – and about 3.5 cm/1½ in long). These are often to be found in supermarkets, but can be bought in cans. Both red and green chillies are available bottled or pickled from ethnic food shops.

If you see a pretty, bell-shaped pepper that's up to 6 cm/2½ in long and coloured green or red, then it is likely to be the milder ancho. Its full flavour and relative sweetness make it a favourite in dishes that are low on the Heat Scale.

Preparing fresh chillies

Most books will warn you that the capsicin in chillies is highly irritant to the skin and recommend that you wear rubber gloves when preparing them, or use a knife and fork. The hotter chillies contain more of the essential oil and are therefore more of a threat. Wear gloves for absolute safety and always wash chillies in cold water, especially after they have been cut open, to prevent the fumes rising to your face. Capsicin will irritate the eyes, so always wash your hands straight after preparing them and – when handling very hot chillies – it is best to try to remember to keep the hands away from the face for at least an hour. Wash all knives and surfaces with soapy water.

To prepare fresh chillies, twist off the stems and wash in cold water, then split them in half and remove the seeds.

To peel fresh chillies, split them in half, then bake them in the oven or put them under a hot grill until the skin begins to blister. Plunge the chillies into cold water and peel them.

To control the heat level:
a) soak the chillies in cold salted water for about an hour before peeling, or blanch them by bringing to the boil, then draining and rinsing;
b) leave the chillies whole, without puncturing the skin and remove them when serving the dish;
c) add the number of chillies you would like – or that are specified in the recipe – but slice and remove the seeds from only one;
d) for maximum heat, slice the chillies and leave the seeds in.

It is better to taste as you go, adding little by little until the desired pungency is reached. Always chop chillies very finely when using them in uncooked sauces or salad dishes.
    Chillies are very high in the vitamins A and C, having more vitamin C per gramme/ounce than a Valencia orange.

Dried chillies
Usually red, these can be used in many recipes and will keep well if they are wrapped well to keep out moisture.

To prepare dried chillies, wash them in cold water, remove stems and shake out the seeds. Chop or tear into pieces and soak in warm water to cover for about 1 hour, then either

A selection of heat-making ingredients often used in fiery food:

1 dried Tabasco chillies
2 horseradish
3 American anaheim chillies
4 jalapeño chillies
5 fresh root ginger
6 Szechuan red peppercorns
7 freeze dried green peppercorns
8 dried mirasol chillies
9 white and black peppercorns
10 dried powdered ginger
11 dried ginger root
12 white mustard seed
13 black mustard seed
14 cayenne
15 chilli powder
16 hot paprika
17 coarse grain mustard
18 wasabi (Japanese horseradish)
19 North African chilli paste
20 mustard
21 green peppercorns in brine
22 cayenne chillies

drain and use in the recipe or purée in some of the water to make a paste. You can also blanch dried peppers before use.

Look out for the hontaka, a small dried red chilli from Japan. It is extremely hot and very few are needed for a truly incredible firepower. Cayenne pepper can be substituted.

Canned chillies

These should be drained, rinsed in cold water to remove the brine in which they have been preserved, then treated as fresh chillies, unless they are already sliced and without seeds.

Chilli flakes

These can sometimes be found in local shops or the supermarket. They can be used as they are in cooked dishes, or soaked like dried chillies. They have heat rather than flavour but keep well.

Chilli powder

This is often a mixture of dried ground cayenne chillies and paprika, with other spices such as cumin, cloves, garlic and marjoram. It varies in strength and flavour depending on its country of origin, so it is wise to taste a small quantity when trying out an unfamiliar brand for the first time. It can be used to flavour stews and sauces.

Cayenne

The unadulterated finely ground pods of the hot cayenne chilli, this powder is bright red and extremely hot; use it in place of fresh chillies, but with great caution. Cayenne is the perfect 'hot' garnish for creamy prawn dishes and other seafood concoctions. About ⅛ teaspoon is the equivalent of one of the tiniest, hottest Mexican chillies, the pequín – seldom found abroad.

Paprika

This is the powder made by grinding the dried flesh of the sweet red pepper (*Capsicum anuum*). It is much milder than the identical-looking cayenne and you'll find brands labelled sweet, hot, mild or Hungarian. To spice your paprika to Hungarian standards, see page 24. Keep it airtight and if possible in a cupboard away from the light, or it loses potency and flavour quite quickly. You can tell by the colour, which fades.

Bottled chilli sauces

Tabasco sauce is probably the best known. Still bearing the name of its co-originator, McIlhenny, it is made of 'spirit vinegar, red pepper (the cayenne chilli) and salt'. A thicker chilli sauce, from Chinese grocers, is used more as a dipping sauce.

Curry powder

Curried dishes are usually seasoned according to personal taste and individual recipe, and different spice combinations are appropriate for the different meats, fish and poultry. Spice up commercially prepared curry powder with cayenne, or make up your own from the recipe below. It is a good Madras-style strength and convenient for the Indian recipes in this book.

5 tbsp hot red chilli powder
½ tsp ground ginger
½ tsp mustard seeds
½ tbsp cloves
5-cm/2-in stick cinnamon
4 tbsp coriander seeds
4 cumin seeds
3 tbsp turmeric
½ tsp fenugreek
½ tsp cardamom

Mix all the ingredients together and grind in a spice mill or blender until fine. Store in an airtight jar.

Europe

The continent of Europe may not be the first one that springs to mind when we think of fiery foods, but there are pungent ingredients to be found. In the north, especially Germany and Scandinavia, liberal use is made of horseradish and mustard, while Hungary, Romania and Czechoslovakia are famous for their paprika-based dishes, and their love of sweet peppers.

Paprika is probably the only true chilli used extensively, although the paprika you most often find in the supermarkets is likely to lack its *capsicin* – the essential fiery oil – and is sweeter and much milder than the Hungarian variety. If you can't obtain Hungarian (sometimes called 'Hot') paprika, make up your own by mixing three parts sweet paprika with one part cayenne or chilli powder, or adjust the seasoning of the dish itself with judicious amounts of cayenne. When using paprika, monitor the temperature of the cooking carefully, as overheating will break down its sugar content and spoil its flavour. In other words, never allow paprika dishes to boil, but always simmer over very low heat.

True hot chillies really surface only in Spanish cuisine, although cayenne pepper, once introduced, became a firm favourite in Britain – as did the fiery hot Tabasco sauce – especially as a seasoning for seafood. France added its distinctive Dijon mustard and use of crushed peppercorns to the pungency stakes. So, although not the 'hottest' of regions, Europe makes a good starting point for our tour of the world's most fiery dishes.

Heat scale 2

Hungarian Onion Soup

Serves 4

Similar to the classic French onion soup, yet with extra bite.

3 large onions, sliced and separated
  into rings
75g/3 oz butter
2 tbsp Hungarian (hot) paprika
1 l/1¾ pt beef stock
3 tomatoes, peeled and chopped
¼ tsp dried oregano
salt to taste

Sauté the onions in the butter until soft and golden-brown. Add the paprika and fry, stirring constantly, for 2 minutes. Add the remaining ingredients, lower the heat and simmer gently for 2 hours.

Serve with a tossed green salad and slices of dark rye bread as a light supper or hearty lunch dish.

Courgettes with Dill, Hungarian Onion Soup, Steak aux Trois Poivres

Heat scale 2

Hungarian Cream of Vegetable Soup

Serves 4–6

The Hungarians enjoy their vegetables in creams or sauces, as this recipe shows. A variety of vegetables can be used in combination, or make it as a single vegetable soup.

1 medium onion, chopped
2 stalks celery, chopped
1 l/1¾ pt chicken stock
450g/1 lb chosen vegetables (carrots, potatoes, green beans etc.), coarsely chopped
2 tbsp flour
2 tbsp Hungarian (hot) paprika
4 tbsp water
6 tbsp double cream
salt and freshly ground black pepper

Simmer the onion and celery in the stock until they are tender. Remove and purée in a blender or food processor, or work through a sieve until smooth. Return to the heat, add the vegetables and continue simmering until they are tender, about 20 minutes.

Mix the flour and paprika, then stir into the water to make a paste. Stir this into the soup mixture and heat until the soup thickens. Remove from the heat and slowly stir in the cream. Return to the heat and simmer for 5–10 minutes, or until heated through. Take care not to let it boil or the cream will curdle. Adjust the seasoning to serve.

Heat scale 1

Marinated Spiced Prawns

SPAIN

Needs advance preparation

Serves 4

The combined pungencies of mustard and horseradish result in a surprising seafood dish that would be served as *tapa* or hors d'oeuvre in a local pavement café or tapas bar. If uncooked prawns are hard to find, use scallops or the largest cooked shelled prawns you can find.

450g/1 lb Dublin Bay prawns, preferably uncooked, shelled
300–450ml/½–¾ pt water
1 tbsp pickling spice
1 tbsp Dijon mustard
2 tbsp Creamy Horseradish Sauce (page 27)
3 tbsp olive oil
4 spring onions, trimmed and chopped
½ tsp salt

If using uncooked prawns, make a shallow cut down the back of each and remove the fine digestive cord that runs down the back. Wash the prawns well. Put them in a pan with the water and pickling spice, bring to the boil and simmer gently for 1½ minutes. They should look opaque when cooked. Drain.

Combine the rest of the ingredients and toss the prawns in the mixture until well coated. Marinate overnight.

Serve on a bed of chopped fresh spinach.

Note if using *cooked* prawns, bring to the boil, then leave to cool in the spicy water before draining.

Rouille

Hot Sauce

FRANCE

No book on hot food would be complete without a mention of this surprising 'condiment' from the Mediterranean coast of France. It is fiery hot, and a little is used to add pungency to the classic fish broths of the region. Try a little spread on croûtes of bread and dropped into a broth of your choice.

2 slices white bread, crusts removed
a little water (see method)
2 red chillies, seeds removed,
    chopped
4 cloves garlic, crushed
1 egg yolk
salt
150ml/¼ pt olive oil

Soak the bread in a little water and squeeze to a pulp. Work together the chilli, bread, garlic, egg yolk and salt, and whisk in a little of the oil. Gradually whisk in the rest of the oil and taste for seasoning.

Serve stirred into the soup, or spread on small pieces of toast.

Creamy Horseradish Sauce

Heat scale 2

HUNGARY

Makes about 300ml/½ pt

This basic sauce recipe can be used in other recipes, or as an accompaniment to plain roast meats, such as beef or ham, or with fish fillets.

25g/1 oz butter or margarine
2 tbsp flour
¼ tsp salt
6 tbsp chicken stock
4 tbsp grated fresh horseradish
150ml/¼ pt double cream

Melt the butter or margarine in a saucepan and stir in the flour and salt. Cook for about 2 minutes, but do not allow the flour to brown. Stir in the stock and horseradish and heat gently. Slowly add the cream, stirring constantly. Cook until thickened and smooth, without allowing the sauce to boil.

Spanish Pepper Salad

Heat scale 2

Serves 4

This recipe is unique because it contains four different varieties of *capsicum* (pepper) used in diverse ways within the context of a single dish. The chillies are used for taste and heat, the sweet peppers just for taste, and the pimentos and paprika provide colour as condiments and garnishes.

The dressing

¼ tsp made mustard
6 tbsp olive oil
2 tbsp red wine vinegar
2 cloves garlic, crushed
salt and freshly ground black pepper
*   to taste*

The salad

100g/4 oz rice (or 350g/12 oz cooked
*   rice)*
2 green or red chillies, skinned, seeds
*   removed, chopped*
1 tsp paprika
1 green or red pepper, cored, seeds
*   removed, sliced*
2 tomatoes, skinned and chopped
1 tbsp chopped fresh parsley
2 tbsp cooked peas
50g/2 oz green olives, chopped
4 canned pimentos, drained and cut
*   into strips*

Put all the dressing ingredients into a screw-topped jar. Replace the lid and shake vigorously until the dressing is emulsified. Taste for seasoning.

Cook the rice, if necessary, allow to cool, then toss it with the dressing. Add all the remaining ingredients except the pimento strips, and marinate for 1 hour. Fork through the salad, garnish with the pimento strips and serve at room temperature.

Heat scale 1

Russian Beetroot Salad

Needs advance preparation

Serves 4

1 heaped tbsp grated fresh
*   horseradish*
6 medium beetroot, cooked, skinned
*   and sliced*
1 small onion, sliced and separated
*   into rings*
6 tbsp vinegar
3 tbsp water
4 tbsp brown sugar
¼ tsp caraway seeds
salt to taste
extra onion rings for garnish

A sweetly pungent sauce accents the beetroot in this typical Russian salad.

Mix together all the ingredients and leave to marinate overnight.

Serve garnished with fresh onion rings.

Czechoslovakian Meatballs with green noodles, Russian Beetroot Salad

Hungarian Beef Goulash

Serves 4

This dish can be a meal in itself – just add cooked potatoes and other vegetables before serving. It is simple to prepare and a good stew for a slow-cooker.

450g/1 lb chuck steak, cubed
50g/2 oz flour
3 tbsp oil
1 large onion, chopped
1 clove garlic, crushed or finely
   chopped
3 tbsp Hungarian (hot) paprika
50g/2 oz mushrooms, sliced
450ml/¾ pt beef stock
salt to taste
250ml/8 fl oz white wine

Coat the beef cubes in the flour and brown on all sides in the oil. Remove the meat and transfer to a large saucepan or a slow-cooker.

Sauté the onion and garlic in the oil until soft and golden but not browned, then stir in the paprika and heat for a further 2 minutes. Add this mixture to the meat with the mushrooms. Pour in the stock, season with a little salt if necessary, and simmer for about 2 hours, stirring occasionally. Stir in the wine about 5 minutes before serving.

Serve with ribbon noodles or potatoes baked in their jackets and a green vegetable such as broccoli or beans.

Variations Just before serving, add 150ml/5 fl oz soured cream – a Western adaptation, but still good. For more heat, add a sprinkling of cayenne.

Steak aux Trois Poivres

Needs advance preparation

Serves 4

2 tbsp black peppercorns
1 tbsp green peppercorns
2 tbsp white peppercorns
4 fillet or sirloin steaks, at least
   2.5 cm/1 in thick
1 tsp salt
50g/2 oz butter
3 tbsp Worcestershire sauce
1 tsp Tabasco sauce (optional)
3 tbsp brandy

FRANCE

Three different types of pepper are called for in this recipe, but the steak is excellent just with crushed black peppercorns.

Wrap all the peppercorns in a cloth and crush with a pestle, hammer or meat bat. Grinding them in a peppermill makes the pepper too fine. Coat the steaks on both sides with crushed peppercorns, pressing them well in with a rolling pin or the base of a bottle. Leave the steaks, uncovered, at room temperature, for at least 1 hour.

Sprinkle the salt in a large frying pan and heat until the base is very hot and the salt begins to brown. Sear the steaks very quickly on each side. Add the butter and cook the steaks for 1 minute on each side, then add the Worcestershire sauce and Tabasco sauce and continue cooking for 1–3 minutes a side, depending on thickness and how well-done you like your steak. (Traditionally, they should be fairly rare.)

Pour the brandy over the steaks, wait 10 seconds, then set alight. When the flame dies out, transfer the steaks to a warm serving dish. Reduce the pan juices and pour over the steaks to serve.

Serve with sauté potatoes, or chips, and a fresh spinach salad.

Variation For a thicker sauce, add 3–4 tablespoons cream to the pan juices after removing the steaks.

Fondue Bourguignonne

SWITZERLAND

Although not the traditional fondue, which is cheese, this recipe is fun, especially when you experiment with your own sauce variations. With this dish, each individual uses a fondue fork to fry the steak cubes in the oil at the table. The sauces are used for dipping according to taste and desired pungency.

225g/8 oz top-quality fillet or sirloin steak per person, cut in even-sized 2.5-cm/1-in cubes
garlic salt
peanut (groundnut) oil for cooking
100g/4 oz butter

Season the cubed beef with garlic salt. Heat enough peanut (groundnut) oil to fill the fondue pot one-third to half full. Heat until it reaches 190°C/375°F on a cooking thermometer, remove from the stove and add the butter. Cover until ready to serve.

When ready to eat, re-heat the oil mixture in the fondue pot until a 1-cm/½-in cube of bread browns in 50 seconds. Transfer the pot to a burner on the table so that each person can cook their steak cubes. When cooked, transfer each piece of meat to a second (cool) fork and dip in one of the following sauces.

Heat scale 2

Makes about 600ml/1 pt

1 medium onion, chopped
1 small celery stalk, finely chopped
25g/1 oz butter
1 tbsp curry powder, or to taste
½ tsp ground ginger
2 tbsp flour
450ml/¾ pt chicken stock

Curry Sauce

Sauté the onion and celery in the butter until tender. Add the curry powder, ginger and flour and cook, stirring constantly, for 2 minutes. Add the stock and continue stirring until the mixture thickens. Cook over low heat for 5 minutes. Remove and serve.

Curried Mayonnaise

Heat scale 1

Makes about 200ml/¹⁄₃ pt

2 tsp curry powder
¹⁄₄ tsp dry mustard
200ml/¹⁄₃ pt mayonnaise
1 tsp lemon juice
2 hard-boiled eggs, chopped
salt to taste

Combine all the ingredients and let them sit for about 20 minutes for the flavours to blend and mellow.

Mustard Sauce

Heat scale 1

Makes about 200ml/¹⁄₃ pt

2 tsp dry mustard
2 tsp Dijon mustard
2 tbsp cider vinegar
200ml/¹⁄₃ pt mayonnaise

Combine all the ingredients and let them sit for 20 minutes for the flavours to blend and mellow.

Horseradish Sauce

Heat scale 1

Makes about 200ml/¹⁄₃ pt

2 tbsp grated fresh horseradish or
  1 tbsp dried flakes
2 tbsp chopped chives
1 tsp lemon juice
200ml/¹⁄₃ pt soured cream
salt to taste

Combine all the ingredients, taste and adjust the seasoning.

Czechoslovakian Meatballs

Heat scale 2

Serves 4 as a main course

1 medium onion, chopped
2 cloves garlic, chopped
50g/2 oz butter
450g/1 lb minced beef
6 tbsp fresh brown or white
  breadcrumbs
1 egg, lightly beaten
2 tbsp flour
3 tbsp Hungarian (hot) paprika
250ml/8 fl oz beef stock
salt and pepper to taste
150ml/¹⁄₄ pt soured cream

These can be served as a main course or as an hors d'oeuvre.

Sauté the onion and garlic in half the butter until soft. Mix into the meat and breadcrumbs, and bind with the beaten egg. Shape into meatballs.

Fry these carefully in the remaining butter until brown, then remove and drain on kitchen paper. Add the flour and paprika to the pan and stir until lightly brown. Add the stock to the flour mixture and bring to the boil, stirring. Reduce the heat and simmer until the sauce is thickened. Stir in the soured cream and heat thoroughly. Return the meatballs to re-heat in the sauce before serving.

Serve with ribbon noodles and a green vegetable.

Spanish Pepper Salad, Veal Paprikash with Spätzle

Veal Paprikash with Spätzle

Heat scale 2

HUNGARY

Serves 6

Paprikash is the Hungarian classic that combines paprika, two types of cream – single and soured – and a meat. We have included a recipe for making Spätzle – a type of dumpling that is traditionally served with soups or stews.

1 large onion, chopped
1 large red or green pepper, chopped
3 tbsp Hungarian (hot) paprika
3 tbsp olive oil
25g/1 oz flour
salt and pepper
900g/2 lb pie veal, cubed
6 tbsp water, or more
15g/½ oz butter
6 tbsp single cream
150ml/¼ pt soured cream
freshly ground pepper to taste

To garnish
1 tbsp oil
1 tsp paprika

Sauté the onion and pepper with 1 tablespoon of the paprika in the oil until the onion is lightly browned. Season two-thirds of the flour with salt and pepper and dredge the meat in this until coated on all sides. Add to the onions.

Brown the meat on all sides. Add the water and cook until the meat is tender, about 45 minutes, stirring occasionally and adding a little extra water, if necessary. Remove and drain the meat, and reserve the liquor.

Melt the butter, add the remaining flour and 2 tablespoons of paprika and stir to a smooth paste. Heat the mixture, stirring constantly, until it begins to bubble. Remove from the heat and slowly stir in the single cream.

Add the reserved meat liquor and heat to just below boiling point, stirring constantly. Season to taste with pepper, return the meat and simmer for 10 minutes. Stir in half the soured cream, then spoon the rest on top. Heat together 1 tablespoon of oil and 1 teaspoon of paprika, and trickle on top.

Serve with spätzle, or ribbon noodles.

Spätzle

225g/8 oz plain flour
1 egg, beaten
250ml/8 fl oz water
2 tsp salt

Mix together all the ingredients. Drop pea-sized amounts of the dough into boiling salted water to cook. Remove with a slotted spoon when they float to the surface.

Romanian-style Chicken Livers

Heat scale 1

Serves 4

The Hungarian influence is very evident here. Serve the livers on – or with – plain boiled rice and roasted peppers.

1 small onion, chopped
1 clove garlic, crushed or finely
  chopped
75g/3 oz butter

Sauté the onion and garlic in 50g/2 oz of the butter until soft. Add the mushrooms and sauté for an additional 2 to 3 minutes. Remove the onion, garlic and mushrooms from the pan.

100g/4 oz mushrooms, sliced
450g/1 lb chicken livers
2 tbsp flour
1½ tbsp Hungarian (hot) paprika
6 tbsp chicken stock
4 tbsp dry red wine or dry sherry
100ml/4 fl oz soured cream

Add the chicken livers and sauté in the pan, adding the rest of the butter. Mix the flour and paprika and add to the livers so as to cover each piece. Add the stock and simmer until the livers are done, about 15 minutes. Reduce the heat and return the onion, garlic and mushrooms to the pan. Stir in the wine or sherry and soured cream, taking care not to let the mixture boil.

Roasted Peppers

Heat scale 1

Serves 4

Serve hot as a vegetable accompaniment.

4–6 red or green peppers
olive oil
salt

Wipe the peppers, but do not core or remove seeds. Pack them tightly into an ovenproof baking dish and pour over olive oil to coat them thoroughly. Sprinkle with salt and bake at 180°C/350°F/Gas mark 4 for 25–30 minutes, turning once.

Chicken Paprikash

Heat scale 2

HUNGARY

Needs advance preparation

Serves 4–6

A variation on the classic dish, which takes more time to prepare. Use the giblets (if any) to make the stock.

2kg/4-lb oven-ready chicken, giblets removed
4 tbsp Hungarian (hot) paprika
25g/1 oz butter
1 large onion, thinly sliced and separated into rings
2 tbsp flour
250ml/8 fl oz white wine
250ml/8 fl oz chicken stock
150ml/¼ pt soured cream
salt and pepper to taste

Rub the chicken with 2 tablespoons of the paprika and set aside for 2–3 hours. At the end of this time set the oven at 230°C/450°F/Gas mark 8.

Melt the butter in a small saucepan. Place the chicken on a rack in an ovenproof casserole or roasting tin, baste with half the melted butter and cover with the onion rings. Place in the pre-heated oven and immediately turn down the heat to 180°C/350°F/Gas mark 4. Roast the chicken, basting frequently, for 1½ hours until done. Take out the chicken and keep hot.

Add the rest of the butter to the juices in the tin. Stir in the flour and the remaining 2 tablespoons paprika and cook, stirring, for 2–3 minutes. Add the wine and stock, bring to the boil, then turn down the heat and simmer until the mixture thickens. Slowly add the soured cream, stirring constantly, until heated through. Return the chicken to the casserole or tin, cover with the sauce, add salt and pepper to taste, and serve.

Rabbit with Mustard

Heat scale 1

FRANCE

Serves 4

This elegant dish combines the world-famous French mustard with a rich, creamy wine sauce.

4 boneless rabbit pieces
100g/4 oz butter
450ml/³/₄ pt chicken stock
250ml/8 fl oz white wine
2 tbsp flour
salt to taste
250ml/8/fl oz single cream
2 tbsp Dijon mustard
50g/2 oz grated Parmesan cheese

Sauté the rabbit pieces in half the butter in a frying pan until lightly browned. Mix the stock and wine, and pour over the rabbit. Cover and simmer until the rabbit is tender, about 1 hour. Transfer the rabbit pieces to a flameproof gratin dish.

Melt the rest of the butter in a saucepan, add the flour and salt, and stir to a pale, straw-coloured paste, but without allowing the flour to turn brown. Stir in the cream and the mustard and continue cooking over low heat until thick. Spread the sauce over the rabbit in the gratin dish and sprinkle with grated Parmesan cheese. Place under a pre-heated hot grill until the cheese begins to brown.

Serve with green beans, asparagus and duchesse potatoes.

Spaghetti Carbonara

Heat scale 3

ITALY

Serves 2 as a main course

The trick to this 'Roman' dish is to organize all the ingredients and keep them hot. The heat of the ingredients will cook the eggs and make the sauce.

2 eggs
75g/3 oz grated Parmesan cheese
10 streaky bacon rashers, trimmed
1 tbsp red pepper flakes or crushed
  dried red chillies
225g/8 oz spaghetti
salt
1 tsp oil
50g/2 oz butter, softened

Beat together the eggs and half the cheese. Set aside.

Cook the bacon until crisp, remove from pan, drain and crumble. Pour off the bacon fat until 4 tablespoons remain. Add the red pepper flakes or crushed dried chillies to this and heat through.

Cook the spaghetti in plenty of salted boiling water – add 1 teaspoon oil to prevent the pasta from sticking together – until tender but still with some 'bite'. Drain quickly, transfer to a warm serving dish. Add the butter and toss. Next, pour the bacon fat and pepper mixture over the spaghetti and toss until well coated. Add the egg mixture and toss again until thoroughly mixed. Top with the crumbled bacon and the rest of the cheese, and serve at once.

Hungarian Baked Potatoes, Hungarian Cream of Vegetable Soup, Rabbit with Mustard

Serve as a 'typical' Italian meal with a tossed green salad and plenty of garlic bread.

Variation For a creamier sauce, slowly stir 150ml/5 fl oz double cream into the bacon fat/pepper mixture.

Heat scale 1

Baked Fish with Mustard Sauce

YUGOSLAVIA

This simple fish goes well with a rice pilaf and minted carrots.

Serves 4

The fish
450g/1 lb white fish fillets (sole, plaice, cod) or fish steaks
salt and pepper
a little water

The sauce
25g/1 oz butter
2 tbsp flour
¼ tsp salt
1 tbsp dry mustard
1 tbsp water
250ml/8 fl oz chicken stock
a sprinkling of caraway seeds

To bake the fish, set the oven at 180°C/350°F/Gas mark 4. Wipe the fish fillets and set them in a single layer in an ovenproof gratin dish or baking dish. Sprinkle with salt and pepper and pour over just enough water to moisten. Cover and bake in the pre-heated oven for 15–20 minutes, until the flesh is opaque when tested with a fork or the point of a knife.

While the fish is baking, make the sauce. Melt the butter, stir in the flour and salt. Cook over a low heat, stirring, until the flour is lightly browned. Mix the mustard with the water and add this to the stock. Slowly add the flavoured stock to the flour mixture in the pan. Simmer, stirring constantly, until thick. Pour over the baked fish fillets, garnish with the caraway seeds and serve.

Heat scale 2

Salmon with Horseradish

GERMANY

Horseradish is the most common pungent ingredient in the cooking of northern Europe and Scandinavia.

Serves 4

1 potato, peeled and chopped
1 small onion, chopped
1 carrot, peeled and diced
450ml/¾ pt water
2 tbsp flour
½ tsp salt
25g/1 oz butter
150ml/¼ pt single cream
4 salmon fillets or steaks
2 tbsp grated fresh horseradish

Simmer the vegetables in the water until very soft. Remove and drain, reserving the liquid.

Sauté the flour and salt in the butter for a couple of minutes, taking care not to let the flour brown. Mix the cream into the vegetable water and stir this into the flour mixture. Bring the sauce to a boil, add the fish, reduce the heat, and simmer until the fish is cooked, about 15 minutes.

Transfer the fish to a heated serving dish and spread the horseradish over it. Pour the sauce over the fish and serve.

Serve with a hot potato salad and asparagus spears.

'Hot' Cheese Fondue

Heat scale 2

SWITZERLAND

Makes about 900ml/1½ pt

We have added Tabasco to this traditional Swiss dish. To connoisseurs, the best part of this fondue is the thick residue at the bottom of the pot.

50g/2 oz butter
4 tbsp flour
salt to taste
250ml/8 fl oz beer
250ml/8 fl oz milk
1 tsp Tabasco sauce
½ tsp paprika
4 tsp dry mustard
450g/1 lb Gruyère cheese, grated
1 loaf of day-old French bread, cut into cubes

Melt the butter in a saucepan, stir in the flour and salt, and cook for 2 minutes. Stir in the beer and milk and simmer gently until slightly thickened. Stir in the Tabasco sauce, paprika and mustard. Gradually add the cheese, stirring constantly until it melts, taking care not to let it boil. Transfer to a fondue dish and dip the bread cubes, skewered on fondue forks, into the fondue. Transfer to table forks to eat!

Hungarian Baked Potatoes

Heat scale 2

Serves 4

This dish adds colour as well as a little spice to a meal. The potatoes need baking in advance.

1 large onion, chopped
1 tbsp oil
2 tbsp Hungarian (hot) paprika
4 potatoes, baked in their skins
50g/2 oz butter
3 tbsp milk or cream

Sauté the onion in the oil until soft. Add the paprika and fry until the onion is golden brown.

Remove the potatoes from their skins and save the skins. Mash the potatoes with the butter and milk and mix in the onion mixture. Re-stuff the skins with the potato mixture, then heat and serve.

Courgettes with Dill

Heat scale 1

YUGOSLAVIA

Serves 4

Serve hot as a vegetable accompaniment, or cold as a salad.

1 medium onion, chopped
2 tbsp oil
450g/1 lb courgettes, trimmed and sliced
1 tsp dill seeds
1 tbsp Hungarian (hot) paprika
6 tbsp soured cream

Sauté the onion in the oil until soft but not brown. Add the courgettes and dill seeds. Cover and cook over low heat until the courgettes are cooked but still crisp. Mix the paprika into the soured cream, add to the vegetables, heat and serve.

Serve with plain roast meat – beef, chicken or turkey.

Africa and the Middle East

The hot foods of this part of the world are based mostly on chillies. Here are recipes from places as diverse as the southern and eastern shores of the Mediterranean, from Ghana, Nigeria, Ethiopia, and Israel.

Africans love their chillies as hot as possible, as can be seen in the recipes that follow. Cayenne is a chilli cultivated extensively in Africa, and it is used in the super-hot curries that Africans borrowed from the Indian immigrants. Ginger and black pepper make their appearance too, as do spices such as cumin, nutmeg and cloves. One of the most interesting food combinations found in Africa is chilli and peanuts, which appears commonly in dishes from west and central Africa.

But it is chilli – in varying forms – that reigns supreme. Enjoy the skewered meat of Morocco, a typical Tunisian *tajine*, a spicily hot prawn dish from Mozambique, or a falafel from Israel.

Tunisian Shourba

Heat scale 3

Hot Soup

Serves 4–6

Serve this soup with crusty French bread and a crisp mixed salad for a hearty lunch.

700g/1½ lb beef, cut in 1-cm/½-in cubes
1 large onion, finely chopped
4 tbsp olive oil
2 tbsp tomato paste
4 tsp crushed or finely chopped red chillies
1 l/1¾ pt beef stock
salt to taste
50g/2 oz pasta (shells, short macaroni or vermicelli)
1½ tsp lemon juice

Sauté the meat and onion in the oil for 5 minutes, stirring frequently. Add the tomato paste, chillies, stock and salt. Cover and simmer for 1 hour or until tender. Add pasta and extra water, if necessary, and cook until the pasta is tender. Just before serving, add the lemon juice.

Avocado and Chilli Salad, Tunisian Shourba, Falafel

Nigerian Groundnut Soup

Heat scale 4

Serves 4

Peanuts are a large export crop in Nigeria, where they are called groundnuts. This recipe is an unusual combination of peanut butter and chillies made into a soup.

750ml/1¼ pt chicken stock
2 carrots, diced
1 medium onion, chopped
2 hot red chillies or ¼ tsp cayenne
salt to taste
225g/8 oz smooth peanut butter

Combine the stock, carrots and onion in a saucepan and bring to the boil. Reduce the heat and simmer, partially covered, for an hour.

Purée the soup in a blender or food processor until smooth and then return it to the pan. Bring to the boil, add the chillies or cayenne and salt. Cover and simmer for 40 minutes.

Mix the peanut butter with a little of the soup until smooth. Stir this mixture into the soup and simmer for 10 minutes. Remove the chillies, if using, and serve.

South African Peach Chutney

Heat scale 4

Makes about 450g/1 lb

Chutneys are served with meat and poultry dishes. Apparently of Indian origin, many different variations appear from former British colonies, often as part of curry dishes. Not all have this firepower, but many, like the dish below, combine fruit and the pungency of chillies.

175g/6 oz dried peaches, chopped
2 tbsp sugar
175ml/6 fl oz white wine vinegar
1 large onion, chopped
2 cloves garlic, finely chopped
450ml/¾ pt water
175g/6 oz blanched almonds,
  crushed
2 tsp ground coriander
2 tsp hot dried red chillies, crumbled,
  or ¼ tsp cayenne
2.5-cm/1-in piece fresh ginger root,
  peeled and minced

Combine the peaches, sugar, vinegar, onion, garlic and water in a pan and bring to the boil, stirring constantly. Reduce the heat and simmer for 30 minutes, or until the mixture is thick and the peaches are soft. Add the rest of the ingredients and cook for a further 5 minutes.

Cool to room temperature before serving. This chutney will keep for a month, covered, in the refrigerator.

Variation Substitute apricots for the peaches.

Berberé

Heat scale 8

Ethiopian Red Chilli Paste

Makes about 300ml/½ pt

This exotic, fiery hot paste is a curry-like version of similar recipes from Latin America (page 118) and South-east Asia (page 86). It can be used in recipes from Africa and the Middle East where a strong heat source is needed.

3 tbsp chopped onion
3 cloves garlic, chopped
2 tbsp oil
50g/2 oz red chilli powder
1 tsp ground ginger
½ tsp each ground cardamom,
*   cloves, allspice, nutmeg,*
*   cinnamon*
2 tbsp flour
250ml/8 fl oz water

Sauté the onion and garlic in the oil until soft and then mash them in the pan with a fork. Add the chilli powder, spices, and flour. Sauté the mixture over a low heat until it is thoroughly mixed and heated, adding more oil if necessary. Slowly add the water and blend until a very thick sauce or paste forms.

Serve with kitfo, which is raw minced beef mixed with chopped raw onions and spices. The raw meat is dipped in the Berberé and eaten. Berberé can also be used as a dip or a sauce for cooked meats such as chicken or beef.

Falafel

Heat scale 3

ISRAEL

Makes about 36

These are served as hors d'oeuvres or the mixture can be used as a sandwich filling. They are popular served in pitta bread 'pockets' with onions, lettuce and tomatoes.

2 tbsp dried red chillies, crushed
450g/1 lb chick peas, cooked
1 large onion, chopped
1 tbsp parsley, chopped
1 clove of garlic, chopped
1 tsp ground cumin
4 matzos, crumbled
2 eggs
100g/4 oz dried breadcrumbs
oil for frying

Place the dried chillies, chick peas, onion, parsley and spices in a blender or food processor. Add the matzo crumbs and eggs and purée until smooth. Form the mixture into balls and roll in the breadcrumbs. Flatten them slightly.

Deep-fry these in hot oil (190°C/375°F) until browned on all sides. Remove and drain.

Salata Mechioua

Heat scale 4

TUNISIA

Serves 4

In Tunisia this 'grilled salad' is served as a summer salad or dip. Traditionally it is prepared outside over clay charcoal braziers (*mechioua*) and pulverized in brass mortars. It is impressive at a barbecue when made in front of the guests.

6 fresh green or red chillies
2 medium onions
3 cloves garlic
4 tomatoes

Do not skin or peel any of the vegetables but place all the ingredients whole over glowing charcoal or under a hot grill, turning occasionally. Grill the vegetables until the skins pop and burn. Remove from the heat and peel all the vegetables. Pulverize or purée to a coarse sauce.

Serve with a loaf of French bread. Tear off pieces of bread and dip them in the sauce.

Ethiopian Lentil Salad

Heat scale 4

Needs advance preparation

Serves 4–6

Ethiopia has been a Christian country since about AD 300. This lentil salad is traditionally served on meatless days during Lent.

3 tbsp red wine vinegar
1 clove garlic, crushed
3 tbsp oil
salt and pepper to taste
225g/8 oz red lentils, cooked
8 large spring onions, chopped
(including green parts)
6 fresh red or green chillies, skinned,
seeds removed, cut in thin strips

Combine the vinegar, garlic, oil, salt and pepper. Heat to just below boiling point and cool to room temperature. Allow to stand for 1 hour, then strain.

Add the lentils, onions and chillies to the dressing, toss well, then marinate at room temperature for at least 2 hours before serving.

Beef and Peppers, Berberé, Ethiopian Lentil Salad

Avocado and Chilli Salad

Heat scale 3

ISRAEL

An unusual salad that combines fruit, vegetables and two kinds of heat.

Needs advance preparation

Serves 4

2 tbsp raisins
a little water
2 tsp crushed red chillies or chilli
   flakes
½ tsp grated ginger root
250ml/8 fl oz orange juice
salt to taste
3 medium carrots, grated
2 avocados

Cover the raisins in water and soak for 30 minutes, then drain. Combine the chillies, ginger, orange juice and salt. Add the carrots and toss until they are well coated. Marinate the mixture for 2 hours in the refrigerator. Peel the avocados and cut them into wedges. Arrange on a plate, top with the marinated carrots, and garnish with the raisins.

Chakchouka

Heat scale 4

TUNISIA

This traditional Tunisian dish could more aptly be called a vegetable hash. It makes an excellent lunch dish.

Serves 4

2 large onions, thinly sliced
3 tbsp olive oil
4 green chillies, skinned, seeds
   removed, cut in strips
2 small hot (serrano) chillies, finely
   chopped, or ¼ tsp cayenne
4 large tomatoes, peeled and sliced
1 red or green pepper, chopped
1 tbsp vinegar
salt to taste
4 eggs

Sauté the onion in the oil until transparent. Add all the other ingredients except the eggs. Simmer this mixture, covered, until the vegetables are very soft.

Make 4 indentations in the vegetables and carefully break an egg into each one. Cover the pan and cook over a low heat until the eggs are well set.

Moroccan Brochettes

Heat scale 3

Serves 4–6

Moroccans love to cook outdoors over charcoal braziers. Roadside stands selling various kinds of grilled meats and crusty flat breads are quite common throughout the country.

4 tsp red chilli powder or ⅓ tsp
   cayenne

Mix all ingredients together. Shape into 5-cm/2-in balls and thread on wooden skewers that have been soaked in water.

900g/2 lb minced beef
2 tbsp finely chopped parsley
1 medium onion, finely chopped
½ tsp ground cumin
1 tsp dried oregano, crushed
salt and pepper to taste

Cook the brochettes over charcoal until done.

Serve over rice, or with couscous, or use as a sandwich filling.

Heat scale 4

Beef and Peppers

ETHIOPIA

Serves 6

Serve this dish with a bowl of Ethiopian Berberé (page 43) on the side. Guests can then adjust the pungency according to taste.

6–7 green chillies, skinned, seeds removed, chopped
2 tsp finely chopped fresh ginger root
4 cloves garlic, chopped
¼ tsp each ground cardamom, turmeric, cinnamon and cloves
6 tbsp red wine
6 tbsp oil
1 kg/2 lb sirloin steak, cut in 1-cm/½-in thick strips
350g/12 oz onions, chopped
2 red or green peppers, cut into strips

Purée the chillies, ginger, garlic, spices and wine to a smooth paste. Heat the oil and brown the beef. When evenly browned, remove and drain off all but 2 tablespoons of oil. Sauté the onion in the oil until soft but not browned. Add the peppers and sauté for 3 minutes more. Add the chilli purée and bring to a boil, stirring constantly. Add the beef and mix until the strips are coated with the sauce. Reduce the heat and simmer for 10 minutes or more until the beef is done.

Serve with rice or boiled potatoes and sliced carrots.

Heat scale 8

Nigerian Beef Kebabs

Needs advance preparation

Serves 4–6

There is a particular partiality for the combination of chillies and peanuts in parts of Africa. The heat of these kebabs is controlled by the amount and type of chillies used – traditionally they are very, very hot.

700g/1½ lb beef steak, cut in 5-cm/2-in cubes
450ml/¾ pt lager or beer
225g/8 oz raw peanuts, shelled and crushed
4 tbsp crushed red chillies or 2 tsp cayenne, or to taste

Marinate the beef in the beer for 3–4 hours, turning occasionally. Mix the peanuts with the chillies or cayenne and roll the beef cubes in this mixture until completely coated. Thread the beef cubes on to skewers and cook over charcoal until done.

Serve with a cucumber salad and glazed carrots, though in Nigeria they are eaten straight off the barbecue or charcoal grill as a starter or first course.

Heat scale 6

Lamb in Peanut Sauce

NIGERIA

Serves 4

Peanut butter and chilli sauces are common in many of the West African stews. The sauce in this recipe is very versatile and can be used with many kinds of meat and poultry.

450g/1 lb lamb, cut in 2.5-cm/1-in
   cubes
3 tbsp oil
water (see method)
40g/1½ oz raw peanuts
2 tsp crushed dried chillies
75g/3 oz peanut butter
¼ tsp ground nutmeg
salt to taste
shredded coconut for garnish

Sauté the lamb cubes in 2 tablespoons of the oil until browned. Barely cover with water, cover, and simmer for 1 hour or until lamb is tender. Drain.

Sauté the peanuts and chillies in the remaining oil for 5 minutes. Add the peanut butter and mix thoroughly. Stir 6 tablespoons water, nutmeg, and salt to taste, into the peanut sauce. Add the lamb, cover and simmer until heated. Garnish with the coconut.

Serve over rice with sliced hard-boiled eggs, sliced fresh pineapple and papaya.

Heat scale 4

Lamb Tajine

TUNISIA

Serves 4

A *tajine* is both a stew and the name of the clay pot in which it is cooked. Many combinations of meats, vegetables and even fruit are used in *tajine*.

450g/1 lb boneless lamb, cubed
1 large onion, chopped
2 tbsp oil
water (see method)
salt to taste
5 green chillies, skinned, seeds
   removed, cut in strips
2 unpeeled potatoes, diced
2 tomatoes, peeled and chopped
100g/4 oz stuffed green olives

Sauté the lamb and onion in the oil until the meat is browned. Barely cover with water and add salt to taste. Cover and simmer for 1 hour or until the meat is tender. Add the remaining ingredients, cover, and simmer until the potatoes are done – about 20 minutes.

Serve over couscous and with French bread.

Ethiopian Ginger Vegetables, Orange Chicken

Heat scale 1

Orange Chicken

ISRAEL

Serves 4

This is one of the milder recipes in this book – but also one of the tastiest. The juicier the oranges, the better the dish.

2 tsp finely chopped fresh ginger root
250ml/8 fl oz orange juice
1 tsp grated orange rind
3 tbsp Cointreau
2-kg/4-lb oven-ready chicken
4–6 tbsp honey
6 tbsp white wine
salt to taste
25g/1 oz flour mixed with 3 tbsp
    water

Mix the ginger, orange juice, orange rind and Cointreau together. Place the chicken, breast-side down, in a roasting tin. Pour the orange juice sauce over the chicken and bake, uncovered, at 180°C/350°F/Gas mark 4, for 30 minutes.

Remove the chicken and baste the breast with honey. Return to the tin breast-side up and bake for 10 more minutes, then pour the white wine over the top of the chicken. Continue baking the chicken, basting frequently with the pan juices, for about 1 hour.

Remove the chicken from the tin and keep warm. Heat the pan juices until boiling and slowly stir in the flour mixture. Continue to stir until the sauce thickens.

Serve carved, with some the sauce poured over the slices. Hand the rest of the sauce round in a sauceboat. Garnish with fresh orange slices and serve with rice and green peas.

Heat scale 3

Galinha Muamba

Angolan Chicken

Needs advance preparation

Serves 4–6

A number of vegetables can be added to 'Angola's National Dish', including chopped carrots, pumpkin, marrows, potatoes or even turnips. Add them when you cook the solids from the marinade.

3–4 fresh red or green chillies,
    skinned, seeds removed, finely
    chopped
½ tsp ground ginger
1 large onion, finely chopped
3 cloves garlic, finely chopped
salt and pepper to taste
200ml/⅓ pt lemon juice
400ml/⅔ pt water
6 tbsp oil
1.5-kg/3-lb oven-ready chicken, cut
    in pieces

Combine the chillies, ginger, onion, garlic, salt, pepper and lemon juice. Add half the water and half the oil, and mix well. Place the chicken pieces in the mixture and marinate, at room temperature, for 3 hours. Remove the chicken and pat dry. Strain the marinade and reserve both the liquid and the rest of the ingredients.

Brown the chicken pieces in the remaining oil, removing them as they brown. Add extra oil if needed. Add the rest of the marinade ingredients and cook until the onion is soft but not browned. Return the chicken to the pan and add 6 tablespoons of the marinade and the remaining water. Partially cover and simmer over low heat for 30 minutes or until the chicken is tender.

Braised Chicken with Chillies

Heat scale 3

GHANA

Serves 4

Fresh tropical fruits such as pineapple, papaya and mango along with baked yams will complement this easily prepared chicken dish.

25g/1 oz butter
1 tbsp peanut (groundnut) oil
1.5-kg/3-lb oven-ready chicken, cut into 8 or 10 pieces
1 onion, sliced and separated into rings
up to 300ml/½ pt chicken stock
½ tsp ground nutmeg
salt and pepper to taste
3–4 green chillies, skinned, seeds removed, chopped

Melt the butter and oil and brown the chicken, a few pieces at a time. As the chicken browns, remove and keep warm. Add the onion rings and sauté until soft.

Add the stock, nutmeg, salt, pepper and chillies and bring to a boil. Put the chicken back in the pan, cover with the stock, adding a little extra, if necessary. Reduce the heat and simmer until the chicken is cooked – about 45 minutes.

Variation Make a stew by adding coarsely chopped onions, tomatoes and sweetcorn kernels while the chicken is simmering.

Mozambique Camarao Piripiri

Heat scale 6

Spicy Prawns

Needs advance preparation

Serves 4–6

In Africa 'piripiri' is used to describe the chillies as well as dishes that contain them. Use scampi, Dublin Bay prawns, or chunks of white fish.

900g/2 lb uncooked Dublin Bay prawns or scampi, peeled and de-veined

Combine the garlic with one-third of the oil and purée in a blender or food processor until smooth. Add the chillies, the rest of the oil and salt to taste.

The marinade
4 cloves garlic, chopped
350ml/12 fl oz oil, peanut (groundnut) preferred
4 tbsp crushed red chillies, or ½ tsp cayenne
salt to taste

Toss the prawns or scampi until completely coated, then marinate them in the refrigerator for 4 hours. Drain and cook the prawns or scampi over charcoal, or under a pre-heated hot grill. Meanwhile, melt the butter and stir in the lemon juice. Add 6 tablespoons of the marinade and pour this sauce over the prawns to serve.

The lemon-butter sauce
50g/2 oz butter
juice of 4 lemons

Ethiopian Ginger Vegetables

Heat scale 4

Serves 6

This casserole can be served as a vegetarian main course as well as a vegetable accompaniment.

6 small potatoes, cubed
225g/8 oz green beans
4 carrots, cut into strips
water (see method)
2 medium onions, quartered and
    separated
5 green chillies, skinned, seeds
    removed, chopped
2 tbsp olive oil
1 tsp fresh grated ginger
2 cloves garlic, finely chopped
salt and pepper to taste

Place the potatoes, green beans and carrots in boiling salted water to cover and cook for 5 minutes. Remove the vegetables and rinse.

Sauté the onion and chillies in the oil until soft but not browned. Add the ginger, garlic, salt and pepper and sauté for 5 minutes. Return the cooked vegetables, stir well, and cook over medium heat until the vegetables are tender but still fairly crisp.

Spicy Carrots

Heat scale 3

TUNISIA

Serves 4–6

Hirsa, which is a mixture of chilli, cumin and salt, is what gives these carrots their 'spice'. This dish is served both hot as a vegetable dish and cold as a salad.

450g/1 lb carrots, cut in matchstick
    strips
water to cover
salt to taste
2 tbsp olive oil
1 tbsp vinegar
½ tsp cumin seeds
2 tsp red chilli powder or ¼ tsp
    cayenne

Simmer the carrots in the water and salt until just tender. Remove from the pan and drain. Toss the carrots in a mixture of the oil and vinegar. Add the remaining ingredients and heat until warm.

Variation Serve cold as a salad.

Spicy Carrots, South African Peach Chutney, Mozambique Camarao Piripiri

The Indian Subcontinent

It goes without saying that India is renowned for its curries, and there are as many recipes for curried dishes as there are cooks in India. Each of the diverse states and cultures that go to make up this teeming subcontinent has its direct influence on the local cuisine. Generally, the curries are cooler in the north, growing progressively hotter with the climate as you travel further south, with the hottest dishes being found on the island of Sri Lanka. For the hotter the combination of spices and the greater the use of chillies, the better the human body can stand the intense, blistering heat.

Here is a sampling of some of the more typical curry dishes. They are really very simple – despite the list of different spices – and serve as an excellent introduction to the subtle art of spicing. Lamb, for instance, needs a different combination of seasonings from either chicken or fish but we have given a good recipe for a basic curry powder on page 23 that is used in several of the recipes that follow. It is, of course, the use of the various chillies that once again ensures the level of heat, together with ginger and a touch of garlic. And if you overdo the chilli heat, remember the best antidote is a spoonful of plain yogurt, quickly administered, to cool the palate for the next onslaught.

Heat scale 3

Indian Split Pea Soup

Needs advance preparation

Serves 4–6

This hearty vegetarian soup is a curry variation of an old favourite.

350g/12 oz split peas
900ml/1½ pt chicken stock or water
3 tsp chilli powder
½ tsp ground ginger
¾ tsp turmeric
1 tsp ground coriander
small bunch spring onions, chopped
  (including green parts)
2 tomatoes, diced
1 tsp cumin seeds, crushed
salt to taste

Wash the split peas and soak overnight. Add the split peas to the stock or water with the chilli powder, ginger, turmeric and coriander. Bring to the boil, reduce the heat and simmer until the peas are done, about 2 hours. Remove from the heat and purée in a blender or food processor until smooth.

Add the remaining ingredients to the purée and simmer for an extra 20 minutes.

Serve for lunch with a salad and crusty bread or rolls.

Mulligatawny Soup

Heat scale 2

Serves 6–8

No book of 'hot' recipes would be complete without Mulligatawny Soup – believed to have been developed by Indian cooks for the British during the Raj. There are many variations; here's ours.

2 medium onions, diced
2 cloves garlic, crushed or finely chopped
2 stalks celery, diced
3–4 carrots, diced
50g/2 oz butter
1½–2 tbsp Curry Powder (page 23)
4 tbsp flour
1.4 l/2½ pt chicken stock
100g/4 oz cooked chicken, diced
1 large cooking apple, peeled and diced
75g/3 oz cooked rice
salt to taste

Sauté the onion, garlic, celery and carrots in the butter until soft. Add the curry powder and flour and heat, stirring constantly to avoid lumps. Add the stock and simmer for 20 minutes. Add the chicken, apple, rice and salt. Cover and simmer for an extra 15 to 20 minutes. Taste for seasoning, then serve.

Variations Stir in 150ml/¼ pt warm cream before serving. Purée the vegetables or strain the stock before adding the chicken and rice. Serve with the cream.

Indian Tomato Chutney

Heat scale 4

Needs advance preparation

Makes about 450ml/¾ pt

Chutneys are Indian counterparts of the hot chilli *salsas*, or sauces, of the West and are usually served with meat, fish and poultry.

6 green chillies, skinned, seeds removed, chopped
4 large tomatoes, peeled and chopped
1 medium onion, chopped
2 cloves garlic, chopped
½ tsp ground ginger
1½ tsp paprika
4 tbsp red wine vinegar
75g/3 oz sugar, or to taste
1 tsp salt

Combine the chillies, tomatoes, onion and garlic in a saucepan. Bring to the boil and simmer until the tomatoes are soft and broken down – about 30 minutes.

Add the remaining ingredients, bring to the boil, reduce the heat, and simmer for an additional 30 minutes. Allow the chutney to set in the refrigerator for 24 hours before serving.

Cold Curry Dressing

Heat scale 2

Makes about 300ml/½ pt

This dressing is especially good to serve with chicken or fish salads. It combines pungency with cool temperatures.

3 tsp Curry Powder (page 23)
1 tsp made mustard
2 tbsp sugar
1 egg, beaten
25g/1 oz butter
25g/1 oz flour
250ml/8 fl oz milk
3 tbsp vinegar
salt to taste

Combine the curry powder, mustard and sugar. Add the egg and stir until smooth. Melt the butter and stir in the flour. Heat for 2 minutes, stirring constantly. Add the milk and curry mixture. Cook the mixture until thickened, stirring constantly. Slowly add the vinegar and salt to taste. Mix well and refrigerate before serving.

Serve cold over meat, poultry or raw vegetables.

Cucumber Raita

Heat scale 3

Cucumbers in Yogurt

Needs advance preparation

Serves 4–6

There are a wide variety of yogurt-based salads or relishes, called *raitas*, in India. They combine spices, yogurt and a variety of vegetables both raw and cooked.

150ml/¼ pt plain yogurt
150ml/¼ pt soured cream
2 heaped tbsp chopped fresh mint
½ tsp ground cumin
2 cucumbers, peeled and thinly sliced
2 small tomatoes, diced
3 green chillies, skinned, seeds
   removed, chopped

Combine the yogurt, soured cream, mint and cumin to make the sauce. Mix together the cucumber slices, tomatoes and chillies. Pour the sauce over and toss the vegetables gently. Chill for 2 hours before serving.

Curried Lamb

Heat scale 5

Serves 4

This is a basic, easy-to-prepare curry that can be dressed up with a wide assortment of accompaniments.

Mulligatawny Soup, Indian Tomato Chutney, Chopped Cucumber and Ginger, Curried Lamb

450g/1 lb boneless lamb, diced
4 tbsp oil
3 onions, chopped
2 tbsp Curry Powder (page 23)
450ml/¾ pt lamb or beef stock
2 tbsp flour mixed with 2 tbsp water
salt and pepper to taste

Brown the lamb in the oil. Add the onion and sauté until soft. Add the curry powder and heat, stirring constantly. Add the stock and simmer until the meat is very tender, about 1 hour. Remove the lamb, reserving the liquid. Slowly pour in the flour mixture, bring to the boil and stir until the sauce has thickened. Replace the lamb, add salt and pepper to taste, and simmer over a low heat until heated through.

Serve the Curried Lamb on a bed of rice with your chosen combination of the following accompaniments: chutney, raw peanuts, raisins, shredded coconut, chopped onions, chopped hard-boiled eggs, chopped apples, chopped bananas, and chopped tomatoes.

Variations For a hotter curry, add cayenne or dried chilli flakes. Substitute chicken for the lamb.

Heat scale 3

Pakistani Lamb

Needs advance preparation

Serves 6–8

Although this fragrant, spicy lamb is a rather elaborate and time-consuming dish, it is well worth it!

3 tsp dried hot chillies
6 tbsp lemon juice
5 cloves garlic, chopped
1 tsp cumin seeds
½ tsp ground cinnamon
⅛ tsp cardamom seeds
1 tsp turmeric
½ tsp ground cloves
¼ tsp salt
a 2-kg/4-lb leg of lamb, trimmed of
    fat and membrane
150ml/¼ pt plain yogurt
100g/4 oz blanched almonds
75g/3 oz raisins
3 tbsp honey
250ml/8 fl oz water
salt to taste

Combine the first nine ingredients in a blender or food processor and purée to a smooth paste. Cut slits in the leg of lamb about 1.75 cm/¾ in apart and 5 cm/2 in deep. Rub the paste into the slits and over the rest of the leg. Set aside at room temperature for 1 hour.

Purée the yogurt, almonds and raisins until smooth. Place the lamb in a casserole, cover with the yogurt mixture, then pour the honey over the top. Cover tightly and marinate for 12 hours or more in the refrigerator.

Add the water and salt to the casserole and cook the lamb at 180°C/350°F/Gas mark 4 for 1½ hours, then reduce the heat to 160°C/325°F/Gas mark 3, and bake for 45 minutes, or until done.

Serve the spicy lamb with a plain vegetable and green salad.

Heat scale 6

Beef Curry

PAKISTAN

Serves 6

Beef is officially served only in northern India and neighbouring countries like Pakistan where the Hindu influence is tempered by Muslims and Christians. A good basic curry – adjust the heat to suit your palate.

1 small onion, chopped
2 tsp coriander seeds
1 tsp ground cloves
2 cardamom seeds
450ml/¾ pt water
4 dried hot chillies, crushed
1 tbsp grated fresh ginger root
2 cloves garlic, chopped or crushed
4 tbsp oil
900g/2 lb lean beef, cut in 2.5-cm/
    1-in cubes
4 tbsp plain yogurt
¼ tsp ground nutmeg

Purée the onion, coriander, cloves and cardamom in 3–4 tablespoons of the water in a blender or food processor until smooth.

Sauté the chillies, ginger, garlic, and the spice mixture in the oil for 2 minutes. Add the beef and fry until browned. Add the rest of the water and simmer, covered, until meat is very tender, about 1 hour. Add the yogurt and nutmeg and stir until well mixed. Simmer for 5 minutes, or until the mixture is heated through.

Heat scale 3

Tandoori Chicken

Needs advance preparation

Serves 4

This is a barbecue favourite from northern India, where the restrictions on meat consumption are not so strict as in the rest of the country. A *tandoor* is a deep clay oven; *tandoori* refers to chicken that is marinated in a spiced yogurt before cooking in the *tandoor*.

3 tsp grated fresh ginger root
2 cloves garlic, minced
4 tbsp plain yogurt
4 chicken breasts
3 tsp chilli powder or ½ tsp cayenne
3 tsp toasted cumin seeds, crushed
2 tbsp oil

Combine the ginger, garlic and yogurt and rub the mixture into the chicken breasts. Marinate for 24 hours in the refrigerator.

Mix the chilli powder or cayenne, cumin and oil together. Pour this mixture over the chicken and grill or barbecue over charcoal until the chicken is done, turning regularly.

Serve with a fresh, tropical fruit salad.

Heat scale 4

Indian Spiced Chicken

Needs advance preparation

Serves 4

This recipe is a typical example of the Indian philosophy of cooking, and there's the classic combination of ginger, onion and garlic with cloves and other spices. The skin is removed from the chicken, then the spice paste is rubbed in so the heat will penetrate into the flesh.

Overleaf: Tandoori Chicken with saffron rice, Cucumber Raita

*1.5-kg/3-lb oven-ready chicken, cut
    into portions
1 large onion, chopped
6 tbsp oil
4–5 whole red chillies
3 tbsp raw shelled peanuts
4 cloves
2 cardamom seeds
2 tsp coriander seeds
2 tsp grated fresh ginger root
4 cloves garlic, crushed
3 tbsp plain yogurt*

Remove the skin from the chicken and trim off any excess fat.

Sauté the onion in 2 tablespoons of the oil until browned. Remove and drain. Grind the chillies, peanuts and cloves with the cardamom and coriander seeds. Combine this powder with the ginger, garlic and onion. Purée the mixture until smooth. Stir in the yogurt. Rub this yogurt mixture over the chicken and marinate in the refrigerator for 12 hours.

Heat the remaining oil and fry the chicken for 15 minutes on each side. Reduce the heat, cover, and simmer for 45 minutes, or until the chicken is tender. Uncover and cook for an extra 10 minutes or until chicken is lightly browned.

Heat scale 4

Fish in Yogurt Sauce

Serves 4

It is important to see that in this recipe the fish is not overcooked, or it will disintegrate and be lost in the sauce.

*4 white fish fillets, skin removed
flour for dredging
6 tbsp oil
1 small onion, chopped
¼ tsp each ground cinnamon, cloves
    and turmeric
150ml/¼ pt plain yogurt
salt to taste
5 fresh green chillies, skinned, seeds
    removed, finely chopped
4 tsp chopped fresh ginger root*

Dredge the fish fillets in the flour and fry in 4 tablespoons of the oil until browned on both sides. Remove and drain.

Add the rest of the oil to the pan and sauté the onion until lightly browned. Add the cinnamon, cloves and turmeric and stir-fry for 2 minutes. Remove, add the yogurt, and purée in a blender to a smooth sauce. Add salt to taste.

Return the sauce to the heat and simmer for 10 minutes. Carefully slide the fillets into the sauce so that they don't fall apart. Cover and simmer only long enough to heat the fish through, about 3 to 4 minutes. Sprinkle the chopped chillies and the ginger on top.

Serve with rice.

Heat scale 6

Shrimp Vindaloo

Needs advance preparation

Serves 4

Vindaloo describes a style of cooking whereby the main ingredient (seafood, chicken or lamb) is marinated for 12 to 24 hours in a vinegar-based sauce with chilli and other spices. The marinated meat is then cooked in the marinade.

Preceding page: Egg Curry, Indian Spiced Peas, Nepalese Boiled Potatoes

3 dried hot red chillies, or hontaka
  (Japanese) chillies, crumbled
3 tsp chopped fresh ginger root
1 medium onion, chopped
4 cloves garlic, chopped
1 tsp ground cumin
2 tsp turmeric
2 tbsp oil
6 tbsp cider vinegar
450g/1 lb uncooked large shrimps,
  Dublin Bay prawns, or scampi,
  peeled and de-veined
50g/2 oz butter

Combine the first eight ingredients and purée in a blender until smooth. Place this sauce in a glass or ceramic bowl, add the raw shrimps, prawns or scampi and toss until well coated. Cover and marinate in the refrigerator for 24 hours.

Sauté the seafood and the marinade in the butter until cooked through.

Heat scale 4

Scrambled Eggs with Ginger

Serves 4

This breakfast dish will open anyone's eyes!

1 tsp finely chopped fresh ginger root
2 medium onions, finely chopped
25g/1 oz butter
6 eggs
3–4 tbsp milk
salt and pepper to taste
4 green chillies, skinned, seeds
  removed, finely chopped

Sauté the ginger and onion in the butter until the onion is soft. Beat the eggs, milk, salt and pepper together and pour into the frying pan with the onion and ginger. Sprinkle the chillies on top and scramble the eggs over a low heat until they are set.

Serve with croissants and fresh melon slices.

Heat scale 2

Egg Curry

Serves 4

This English adaptation of an Indian egg curry makes a good dish for lunch or Sunday brunch.

450g/1 lb onions, finely chopped
50g/1 oz butter
2 tbsp Curry Powder (page 23)
1 tbsp flour
250ml/8 fl oz milk
8 hard-boiled eggs, 6 chopped and
  2 cut into eighths
4 muffins or soft rolls, split and
  toasted
fresh coriander leaves or parsley,
  chopped

Sauté the onion in the butter until soft. Stir in the curry powder and flour and heat for an additional 2 minutes. Slowly add the milk, stirring constantly until the sauce thickens. Add the chopped eggs and heat thoroughly. Pour over the muffins or rolls, garnish with egg pieces and the coriander leaves or parsley, and serve.

Serve with asparagus and a fresh fruit compote.

Sri Lankan Saffron Rice

Heat scale 8

Serves 4–6

Rice dishes in this form, called pilafs, appear all over the world. This is an exotic version from the country formerly called Ceylon, which has one of the most fiery cuisines in the world.

750ml/1¼ pt boiling water
¼ tsp saffron threads
175g/6 oz long-grain rice, rinsed well
25g/1 oz butter
2 tsp finely chopped fresh ginger root
1 tsp black mustard seeds
50g/2 oz unsalted cashew nuts
4 whole cloves
4–5 green chillies, skinned, seeds removed, finely chopped
6 tbsp fresh lime juice
salt to taste

Pour 2–3 tablespoons boiling water over the saffron and allow it to soak for 10 minutes. Cook the rice in 450ml/¾ pint salted boiling water for 10 minutes, then drain.

Melt the butter, add the ginger, mustard seeds, cashews and cloves and fry the mixture, stirring constantly, until the seeds begin to pop. Add the chillies, lime juice, rice, and the rest of the boiling water and stir well. Pour the saffron water over the mixture and return to the boil, stirring once. Cover the pan tightly and cook for about 15 minutes or until the liquid has been asborbed and the rice is tender. Fluff with a fork before serving.

Curried Cauliflower

Heat scale 4

Serves 6

Cauliflower is one of the vegetables most commonly used in Indian cooking. Potatoes may be substituted in this recipe.

2 tbsp oil
½ tsp mustard seeds
1 tbsp fresh ginger root, peeled and finely chopped
¼ tsp cumin seeds
2 medium onions, finely chopped
½ tsp turmeric
1 cauliflower, divided into florets
2 tomatoes, peeled and chopped
½ tsp sugar
4 green chillies, skinned, seeds removed, finely chopped
salt

Heat the oil until very hot and add the mustard seeds, ginger, cumin seeds and onion. Cook for 2 minutes, stirring constantly. Add the turmeric and continue cooking for 5 minutes. Add the cauliflower and stir until the florets are coated with the mixture. Add the remaining ingredients, with a little water if necessary, reduce the heat, and cook until the cauliflower is tender but firm.

Curried Cauliflower, Fish in Yogurt Sauce

Heat scale 6

Indian Spiced Peas

Serves 4

This dish makes an excellent pungent surprise when served as a side dish with a non-spicy meat such as roast beef or pork.

½ tsp cumin seeds
1 tbsp oil
3 dried red (Japanese) chillies
½ tsp fresh ginger root, peeled and minced
¼ tsp turmeric
450g/1 lb fresh or frozen peas
3 tbsp water

Toast the cumin seeds in the hot oil for 1 minute. Add the chillies or cayenne, ginger and turmeric and sauté for an additional 2 minutes. Stir in the peas, add the water, cover and simmer until the peas are done.

Heat scale 6

Nepalese Boiled Potatoes

Serves 4

Like hamburgers in the United States, chips in Britain, or pasta in Italy, these 'hot' potatoes can be found everywhere in Nepal.

½ tsp dry mustard
1 tsp lemon juice
2 tbsp oil (preferably peanut)
3 potatoes, boiled and cut in 2.5-cm/1-in cubes
2 tbsp crushed red chillies or ½ tsp cayenne

Thoroughly mix the mustard, lemon juice and oil. Pour the mixture over the hot potatoes. Toss gently to coat all the pieces. Sprinkle the red chilli or cayenne over the potatoes and serve.

Serve with plain roast meats and plainly boiled or steamed vegetables – these potatoes can be very pungent.

The Orient

When it comes to the subtle use of spices and chillies, no other cuisine can really match those of China and Japan for delicate but fiery combinations of taste. To the chillies – and combinations of two or more types are often found – are added flavoured oils (sesame and peanut), the distinctly savoury soy sauces, fresh root ginger, and Szechuan peppercorns. These, despite their sharp and spicy taste, are in fact the dried berries of a shrub of the citrus family and not a true pepper at all.

It is widely – and wrongly – believed that dishes from the Hunan and Szechuan provinces are too hot to eat. Remember that the aim is to combine 'heat' with subtle flavour, rather than to obscure the taste, and if properly prepared, even the hottest dishes will be full of flavour. Since you can always make the dish more fiery simply by adding more chillies, start with half the quantity (especially if working with the fiendishly hot hontaka, or Japanese, chillies) then test for pungency, and add more 'heat' as required.

Our selection includes dishes from China, Japan, Korea, and one from almost every point on the Heat Scale. There's the famous Mongolian Fire Pot with its fiery dipping sauces and the pleasantly pungent Korean Short Ribs. Most of the recipes can be cooked in a wok. If you are wok-less, use a large frying pan with a lid.

Heat scale 5

Korean Cucumber Salad

Needs advance preparation

Serves 4

Salt
1 cucumber, thinly sliced
1½ tbsp finely chopped red chilli
2 cloves garlic, finely chopped
3 tbsp rice wine vinegar
1 tbsp sugar
2 tbsp oil
1 medium onion, thinly sliced and
  separated into rings

Cucumber and chilli is a combination that appears in many cuisines throughout the world. This recipe is typical.

Liberally salt the cucumber slices and set aside for 1 hour. Rinse well with cold water and drain.

Mix the chilli, garlic, vinegar, sugar and oil together. Arrange the cucumber and onion in a bowl and pour the dressing over them. Marinate in the refrigerator for 2 hours before serving.

Heat scale 3

Hot Ginger Spinach Salad

CHINA

Serves 4

Summer days in the Szechuan and Hunan provinces can be extremely hot. During such heat people prefer fresh vegetables and salads to meat dishes.

The dressing

3 tsp finely chopped red chilli, or
  ½ tsp chilli powder or cayenne
2.5-cm/1-in piece fresh ginger root,
  peeled and minced or finely
  chopped
2 tbsp light soy sauce
3 tbsp oil (sesame preferred)
1 tsp sugar
¼ tsp salt

For the dressing, heat all the ingredients and keep warm until ready to serve.

For the salad, combine the spinach and onions in a large bowl. Pour the hot dressing over the spinach, toss and serve immediately.

The salad

450g/1 lb fresh spinach, torn into
  bite-size pieces
4 spring onions, chopped (including
  green parts)

Heat scale 4

Spicy Chinese Salad

Serves 4–6

This salad may be served either hot or cold as a separate course after the main course.

2 carrots,, cut into matchstick strips
2 turnips, cut into matchstick strips
water (see method)
1 tsp salt
1 cucumber, cut into matchstick
  strips
½ medium onion, cut into thin
  wedges and separated
1 clove garlic, finely chopped
4 dried red chillies, broken into
  pieces
1 tbsp rice wine vinegar
2 tsp sugar
2 tbsp oil

Soak the carrot and turnip in cold water to cover for 15 minutes. Drain and dry. Salt the cucumber and set aside for 15 minutes. Rinse and dry. Stir-fry all the ingredients in the hot oil for 2 minutes. Let the mixture cool to room temperature and chill in the refrigerator for 1 hour before serving.

Spicy Chinese Salad, Mustard Chicken Shreds

Kim Chee

Heat scale 4

Korean Pickled Cabbage

Kim Chee is a national dish in Korea. There are many variations on this fermented 'salad' – we have included a milder one.

Needs advance preparation

Serves 6–8

salt
1 head Chinese leaves, coarsely
 chopped
4–5 fresh green chillies, skinned,
 seeds removed and finely chopped
2 tsp grated fresh ginger root
6 spring onions, chopped (including
 green parts)
1 clove garlic, crushed
water to cover

Salt the cabbage and set aside for 1 hour. Rinse well with cold water and drain. Add the remaining ingredients to the cabbage and cover with water. Allow the mixture to pickle in the refrigerator for 2 to 4 days. To serve, drain off the water and warm to room temperature.

Serve with grilled meats.

Chilli Oil

Heat scale 9

CHINA

You can buy ready-made chilli oil at a Chinese grocer's shop, but it is easy to make for yourself. It will keep indefinitely in the refrigerator. It may turn cloudy, but if left a little while at room temperature it will clear. The addition of chilli oil will add 'fire' to any recipe.

Needs advance preparation

Makes about 450ml/³⁄₄ pt

450ml/³⁄₄ pt oil (peanut preferred)
10 dried red hontaka (Japanese)
 chillies

Heat the oil until hot, add the dried chillies, seeds and all, then cover and cook over low heat until the chillies turn black. Remove from the heat and cool. Cover and leave at room temperature for 8 hours. Strain through muslin or cheesecloth, then cover and refrigerate.

Serve as a dip, or when you want a subtle chilli flavour when frying or sautéing. However, use with caution, as it is *very* pungent!

Mustard Chicken Shreds

Heat scale 2

CHINA

Serves 4

This dish should be served on individual plates to be eaten as a starter or a salad, with chopsticks.

4 tsp dry hot Chinese mustard
2 tbsp wine vinegar
2 tbsp dark soy sauce
2 tbsp peanut oil
4 tsp sugar
2 tsp water
225g/8 oz cooked chicken, cut in
  thin strips
1 egg, lightly beaten
75g/3 oz cornflour
250ml/8 fl oz oil for frying
2 carrots, grated
4 spring onions, chopped (including
  green parts)

Mix the first six ingredients together and set aside. Coat the chicken shreds with beaten egg and then cornflour. Deep-fry the chicken in the oil until crisp. Remove and drain.

Arrange the chicken on top of a bed of grated carrot and pour the sauce over the top. Garnish with the spring onions and serve.

Heat scale 4

Beef with Hot Peppers

CHINA

Serves 4–6

A classic Szechuan dish. Other Oriental vegetables such as bamboo shoots and bean sprouts may be added.

4 tbsp oil (peanut preferred)
450g/1 lb sirloin or rump steak, cut
  thinly across the grain
2 dried hontaka (Japanese) chillies,
  crumbled
1 tbsp light soy sauce
1 tbsp dark soy sauce
2 tsp sugar
2 tbsp rice wine or dry sherry
2 carrots, cut in matchstick strips
100g/4 oz mangetout peas
3 green chillies, skinned, seeds
  removed, cut into strips
2 tsp cornflour mixed with 2 tbsp
  water

Heat the oil in a wok and stir-fry the beef until dry – about 5 to 8 minutes. Remove the meat, and pour off all but 1 tablespoon of the oil. Add the dried chillies and cook until they start to smoke – about 2 minutes. Remove them.

Combine the soy sauces, sugar and wine. Return the meat to the wok, add the soy sauce mixture, and cook for 5 minutes. Add the carrots, mangetout and green chillies and stir-fry for 2 minutes. Slowly stir in the cornflour mixture and heat, stirring constantly, until thick.

Mongolian Fire Pot

A Mongolian fire pot is similar to a beef fondue except that a spicy 'broth' is used to cook the meat instead of hot oil. All the pungency of this dish is found in the dipping sauces. The broth is drunk at the end of the meal. A fondue pot can be substituted for a fire pot.

1l/1¾ pt beef stock
6 spring onions, chopped (including
  green parts)
3 tomatoes, peeled and chopped
450g/1 lb pork or lamb or fillet steak,
  sliced thinly against the grain (or
  combine the different meats)
450g/1 lb Chinese leaves, cut in bite-
  size pieces
450g/1 lb fresh spinach, cut in bite-
  size pieces
100g/4 oz bean curd (tofu), cut into
  bite-size pieces

Combine the stock, onions and tomatoes in a pan and bring to the boil. Reduce the heat and simmer for 20 minutes. Transfer to a fondue or fire pot. Meat and vegetables are then speared with chopsticks or fondue forks and cooked for a couple of minutes in the broth, then dipped in one of the following sauces.

Heat scale 6

Makes 250ml/8 fl oz

3 tbsp Red Chilli Sauce (page 146)
1½ tsp Chilli Oil (page 70)
3 tbsp soy sauce
3 tbsp rice wine or dry sherry
3 tbsp lemon juice
2 spring onions, chopped (including
  green parts)

Chilli-Soy Sauce

Mix all ingredients together in a pan and heat slowly until hot. Simmer for 10 minutes before serving.

Heat scale 2

Serves 4

3 tbsp dry hot Chinese mustard
1 tbsp sesame oil

Mustard-Oil Dip

Mix the mustard with enough water to make a thin paste, then mix in the oil. It is best to make this dip within 30 minutes before serving.

Heat scale 1

Makes 8 tablespoons/4 fl oz

3 tbsp shredded fresh ginger root
3 tbsp red wine vinegar
2 tbsp light soy sauce

Ginger-Soy Dip

Mix ingredients in a serving bowl, cover, and allow to stand at room temperature for at least 10 minutes before serving. This dip will keep for hours at room temperature.

Heat scale 6

Makes 250ml/8 fl oz

3 dried red (Japanese) chillies,
  crumbled
6 tbsp red wine vinegar
6 tbsp dark soy sauce
2 tbsp peanut oil

Hot Vinegar Dip

Combine the chillies, vinegar and soy sauce. Heat the oil until it is hot and pour over the mixture. Stir and serve.

Mongolian Fire Pot with Chilli-Soy Sauce, Ginger-Soy Dip, Mustard-Oil Dip, Hot Vinegar Dip, Chinese leaves and spinach, tofu

Korean Short Ribs

Heat scale 1

Needs advance preparation

Serves 4

The Koreans are quite fond of marinating beef, chicken or pork in soy-based sauces and then grilling or barbecuing the meat at the table.

4 tsp dry hot Chinese mustard
6 tbsp light soy sauce
3 tbsp oil (peanut or sesame preferred)
3 tbsp white vinegar
2 tbsp sugar
4 spring onions, finely chopped (including green parts)
1 clove garlic, crushed
900g/2 lb beef, chicken or pork ribs, cut in small sections

Mix all ingredients together, except the ribs. Score the ribs, place in a bowl and add the marinade, mixing well. Marinate the ribs overnight in the refrigerator.

Grill or barbecue over charcoal, basting frequently with the sauce, until done.

Serve with rice dishes or as a starter to an Oriental meal with multiple courses.

Chinese Beef Curry

Heat scale 2

Serves 4

Compared to its Pakistani counterpart (page 58), this beef curry dish is less pungent and easier to prepare.

3 tbsp Curry Powder (page 23)
2 tbsp oil (peanut preferred)
2 tsp finely chopped fresh ginger root
1 clove garlic, crushed
450g/1 lb steak, cubed (sirloin or fillet preferred)
1 large onion, cut in wedges
1 tbsp light soy sauce
250ml/8 fl oz beef stock
2 tsp cornflour, mixed with 2 tbsp water

Heat the curry powder until hot. Stir in the oil and sauté the ginger and garlic in the mixture. Add the meat and brown. Add the onion and sauté until transparent. Stir in the soy sauce and stock. Cover and bring to the boil. Reduce the heat and simmer until the meat is tender, about 10 minutes. Slowly stir in the cornflour mixture and heat until the sauce is thick, stirring constantly.

Serve with rice, of course, and steamed mangetout peas.

Stir-fried Ginger Beef

Heat scale 3

Serves 4

CHINA

Originating from northern China, this recipe is one of the few beef dishes from a region that serves mostly poultry and pork. Substitute bean sprouts for bamboo shoots, or buy them canned.

2 tbsp soy sauce
2 tsp sugar
1 tbsp rice wine or dry sherry
450g/1 lb lean sirloin or fillet or rump steak, cut in very thin strips
4 tbsp oil
3 tsp crushed red chillies
2 tsp shredded fresh ginger root
2 stalks celery, cut in matchstick strips
50g/2 oz bamboo shoots, drained if canned, shredded
3 tbsp beef stock
2 tsp cornflour mixed with 2 tbsp water
small bunch spring onions, chopped (including green parts)

Mix together the soy sauce, sugar and wine. Toss the beef in the mixture and marinate for 1 hour.

Stir-fry the beef in 2 tablespoons of the oil until browned, then remove and drain. Heat the remaining 2 tablespoons oil, add the chillies, ginger, celery and bamboo shoots. Stir-fry for 2 minutes. Return the beef to the wok, add the stock and slowly stir in the cornflour mixture, stirring until the mixture thickens. Add the spring onions and serve.

Heat scale 6

Barbecued Hot Lamb

MONGOLIA

Needs advance preparation

Serves 4

This recipe combines lamb and chilli oil, which is typical of central Asia.

4 tbsp hot chilli oil, or combine 2 tsp cayenne and 4 tbsp oil
450g/1 lb boneless lamb, cut into 4-cm/1½-in cubes
4 tbsp fresh lemon juice
3 cloves garlic, crushed
¼ tsp salt

Combine all the ingredients in a bowl and marinate for at least 2 hours. Drain the lamb, reserving the marinade for basting. Barbecue the meat on skewers over a hot charcoal fire. Baste and barbecue until done.

Serve over rice or a wheat (bulgar) pilaf.

Heat scale 7

Szechuan Chicken with Peppers and Peanuts

Serves 4

Chicken with Peppers is a famous Szechuan dish. We have incorporated peanuts for added texture. The firepower of the dish, which traditionally is very hot, can be reduced by adding less cayenne.

2 tbsp rice wine
3 tbsp soy sauce
1 chicken, cut into bite-size pieces
3 tbsp cornflour
oil for deep-frying
1 tsp cayenne
1 tsp grated fresh ginger root
50g/2 oz raw peanuts
3 tbsp oil
1 tsp sugar
2 tsp cornflour mixed with 2 tbsp
  water

Mix 1 tablespoon each of the wine and soy sauce. Add the chicken and toss until coated. Coat the chicken with the cornflour and deep-fry until crisp. Remove and drain.

Sauté the cayenne, ginger and peanuts in 3 tablespoons hot oil for 2 minutes. Add the fried chicken, remaining wine, soy sauce and sugar and bring to the boil. Slowly stir in the cornflour mixture and heat until the sauce thickens.

Serve with sweet-and-sour dishes. Traditionally served over rice.

Sashimi and Sushi

Heat scale 2

JAPAN

Serves 2

As simple as they may seem, these two Japanese specialities are not easily prepared. The serving of raw seafood in Japan is regarded as an art, and sushi chefs are apprenticed for many years to learn the precise techniques of preparation and serving. Sashimi is sliced raw seafood; Sushi combines the raw seafood with cold cooked rice. For ease of preparation we have simplified the complicated ritual, and suggest you cook the seafood first. The seafood suggested can be prawns, abalone, scampi, octopus, squid and the following fish: tuna, bream, carp, salmon or mackerel.

2 tbsp powdered wasabi (Japanese
  horseradish)
20 pieces sliced seafood (see method)
4 tbsp very thinly sliced fresh ginger
  root
6 tbsp soy sauce
100g/4 oz cooked rice of a sticky
  consistency

Fish may be sliced into small fillets 4 × 2.5 cm/1½ × 1 in. The prawns or scampi, after peeling and cleaning, may be sliced or served whole. Though traditionally served raw, for less Oriental tastes and greater safety, par-boil the fish and seafood in water with a slice or two of lemon until opaque. Finely slice the tougher sea creatures like squid and octopus.

Reconstitute the wasabi by mixing with a small amount of water. Place equal amounts of soy sauce in two shallow bowls and add the wasabi, adjusting for individual taste, as this variety of horseradish is very pungent.

The seafood may be served as Sashimi by draining it and allowing to cool, then simply dipping it in the sauce and eating it with your fingers or chopsticks. Between pieces, a portion of fresh ginger is consumed.

Kim Chee, wasabi, soy sauce, Sashimi and Sushi made with raw fish

To make Sushi, form the rice into oblong portions 4 × 1 cm/1½ × ½ in. Place the seafood on the rice and, using your fingers, dip the Sushi in the sauce and eat it in one bite. Etiquette for Sushi requires the use of fingers only (no chopsticks) and no nibbling.

Serve with green tea and tempura vegetables.

Braised Chinese Fish

Heat scale 4

Serves 4–6

The fish in this dish is cooked and served whole, which preserves more of the flavour. In selecting a whole fish, be sure the eyes are clear and bright – the sign of a fresh fish. Buy bean curd cakes (tofu) at a Chinese, Indian or Asian grocer.

4 bean curd cakes (tofu), cut in 2.5-cm/1-in squares
salt to taste
900g/2 lb whole white fish (bream, carp, grey mullet)
3 tbsp red chilli powder
2 tsp finely chopped fresh ginger root
6 spring onions, sliced (including green parts)
1 clove garlic, crushed
2 tbsp soy sauce
1 tsp sugar
3 tbsp oil
250ml/8 fl oz chicken stock

Cook the bean curd (tofu) in boiling water for 15 minutes, then drain. Rub salt into the cleaned fish.

Sauté the chilli powder, ginger, onions, garlic, soy sauce and sugar in the hot oil for 2 minutes. Place the fish in the pan or wok and brown on both sides. Add the stock, cover and cook for 15 minutes over a very low heat or until the fish flakes with a fork. Add the bean curd and serve.

Grilled Lobster

Heat scale 8

Needs advance preparation

Serves 4

CHINA

A sweet-and-sour dish is a complement to this very fiery recipe. The heat can be tempered by reducing the amount of chilli oil, but remember to compensate by adding an equal amount of peanut oil.

6 tbsp Chilli Oil (page 70)
6 tbsp rice wine or dry sherry
6 tbsp light soy sauce
450g/1 lb lobster, diced
oil for stir-frying

Combine the chilli oil, rice wine and soy sauce. Add the lobster and toss until well coated. Marinate for 2 hours in the refrigerator. Drain. Stir-fry the lobster in hot oil until done.

Variation Substitute shelled prawns or scampi for lobster.

Szechuan Spiced Noodles

Heat scale 4

Serves 4–6

Noodles in northern China are served like rice in southern China; they are indeed a staple. This dish is prepared in the hot summer when 'cool' food is a welcome treat. Szechuan peppercorns are available at Chinese grocers, or you can use white peppercorns.

1 tbsp Chilli Oil (page 70)
2 tsp finely chopped ginger root
½ tsp Szechuan peppercorns, crushed
1 clove garlic, crushed
3 tbsp dark soy sauce
3 tbsp oil (sesame preferred)
3 tbsp rice wine vinegar
4 tsp sugar
2 tbsp oil (peanut preferred)
450g/1 lb prawns, peeled and de-veined
175g/6 oz cooked pork, cut into strips
2 stalks celery, cut into matchstick strips
450g/1 lb thin egg noodles, cooked
small bunch spring onions, chopped (including green parts)

Combine the chilli oil, half the ginger, the peppercorns, garlic, soy sauce, sesame oil, vinegar and sugar together in a bowl. Set aside.

Heat the 2 tablespoons peanut oil and add the rest of the ginger. Stir-fry the prawns and pork until done, about 10 minutes, and remove. Stir-fry the celery until slightly soft, remove and drain.

Place the noodles on a hot serving dish, add the celery, and top with the prawn mixture. Pour the sauce over the top and garnish with the onions.

Serve this dish as a main course after a clear soup.

Hunan-style Prawns

Heat scale 5

Needs advance preparation

Serves 2–4

Once again shellfish is combined with chilli and ginger – plus black pepper. The pungency in the prawns is caused by lengthy marinating, but it is worth the wait.

2 dried red hontaka (Japanese) chillies, crumbled, or 4 tsp dried red chilli powder
2 tsp grated fresh ginger root
1 tsp Szechuan peppercorns, crushed
3 tbsp rice wine or dry sherry
1 tsp sugar
450g/1 lb uncooked prawns, peeled and de-veined
6 tbsp peanut oil

Combine the first five ingredients in a bowl, add the prawns, mix well, and marinate overnight in the refrigerator. Drain and reserve the marinade.

Heat the oil in a wok until very hot. Add the prawns and stir-fry until done, about 10 minutes. Warm the marinade and serve as a sauce for dipping.

Heat scale 3

Korean Rice

Serves 6

This is the Oriental version of a pilaf.

225g/8 oz pork, diced
2 tbsp oil
3 tsp red chilli powder
4 spring onions, chopped (including
    green parts)
100g/4 oz mushrooms, sliced
225g/8 oz rice, rinsed well
2 tbsp soy sauce
450ml/³/₄ pt chicken stock

Sauté the pork in the oil until no longer pink. Add the chilli powder, onions and mushrooms and heat until the onions are soft – about 5 minutes. Add the remaining ingredients and bring to the boil. Reduce the heat, cover, and simmer for 20 minutes or until the rice is done.

Heat scale 3

Spicy Stir-fried Vegetables

Serves 4–6

This is a simple vegetable dish from northern China that combines ginger and chillies. Other vegetables, or a combination of vegetables, can be used with the basic recipe.

3 tbsp oil
4 dried red chillies, torn into pieces
1-cm/¹/₂-in piece fresh ginger, peeled
    and shredded
¹/₂ head broccoli, broken into florets
¹/₂ head cauliflower, broken into
    florets
175ml/6 fl oz water
1 tbsp cornflour mixed with 3 tbsp
    water

Heat the oil and stir-fry the chillies and ginger for 10 seconds. Add the vegetables and stir-fry for 2 to 3 more minutes. Add the water, bring to the boil, cover and cook until the vegetables are done but still crisp (5 to 8 minutes). Stir in the cornflour mixture and continue stirring until the sauce is thick and clear.

Variation Cashews or peanuts can be added for texture.

Hot Ginger Spinach Salad, Szechuan Spiced Noodles

South-east Asia and the Pacific Islands

The Indonesian islands owe much of their distinctive and varied style of cooking to the traders, immigrants and settlers – among them the Chinese, Arab and Dutch – who came in search of spices.

Chillies are joined by garlic, onion, coconut and peanuts, and the dishes are flavoured with one or another of the fiery hot chilli pastes of the Indonesian cuisine. The word 'sambal' denotes the use of chillies, often sautéed with onion, to provide condiments way up the Heat Scale to be used with care. Dried red Japanese chillies are much in evidence and many of the ingredients in the previous three chapters seem to have found their way into Pacific dishes.

Nasi Goreng is possibly the best-known and is served with 'omelette' strips or fried egg and tomatoes. Echoes of the Orient are found in Singapore Spare Ribs, and Burmese Beef offers the classic Indian combination of chillies, ginger, onion and garlic. Hawaiian Curried Chicken combines curry spices with coconut milk, and the Saté recipe opposite has a touch of peanut reminiscent of African cooking.

Indonesian Chicken Soup

Heat scale 6

Serves 4–6

This chicken soup is so thick it is almost a stew. For a 'soupier' consistency, add more water.

1.5-kg/3-lb oven-ready chicken, cut in portions
2 large onions, sliced
1 l/1¾ pt water
5-cm/2-in fresh ginger root, peeled and chopped
2 tbsp peanut oil
1 tsp turmeric
2 tsp ground coriander

Cover the chicken and half the onions with the water and bring to the boil. Reduce heat and simmer until the chicken is done, about 1 hour. Remove the chicken; strain and save the broth.

Sauté the remaining onions and ginger in the oil until the onions are soft. Stir spices and cayenne to taste, and sauté for 2 more minutes. Add the mixture to the chicken broth, bring to the boil, then reduce the heat and simmer for 20 minutes.

½ tsp ground nutmeg
1 scant tsp cayenne, or 3 dried red hontaka (Japanese) chillies, crumbled
50g/2 oz cooked rice vermicelli
4 spring onions, chopped (including green parts)

Remove the skin from the chicken, pull the meat from the bones and chop or shred it into bite-size pieces. Add the chicken meat and the vermicelli to the broth and heat until the vermicelli is soft. Garnish with the spring onions and serve.

Variations This basic chicken soup can be altered by changing the garnishes and adding ingredients such as cooked prawns and hard-boiled eggs.

Heat scale 4

Beef Saté

INDONESIA

Makes 6–8

These highly seasoned kebabs are made from all types of meat, fish and spicy pastes. They can be large or small and served as a starter or a main course dish. In Indonesia these satés are often eaten at roadside stalls.

5 green chillies, skinned, seeds removed, chopped
4-cm/1½-in piece fresh ginger root, peeled and chopped
1 medium onion, chopped
2 cloves garlic, chopped
2 tbsp grated lemon rind
1 tbsp dark soy sauce
3 tsp ground coriander
1 tsp turmeric
4 tbsp water
3 tbsp peanut oil
250g/8 fl oz coconut cream (page 87)
750g/1½ lb best-quality steak, cut in 5-cm/2-in cubes

The first nine ingredients constitute the spicy paste. Purée them in a blender or food processor until smooth.

Heat the oil and sauté the paste for 4 minutes, stirring constantly. Add the coconut cream and slowly bring to the boil, stirring constantly. Add the meat, reduce the heat and gently simmer until the meat is tender, about 30 minutes.

While the meat is cooking, soak wooden skewers in water to prevent them from burning during cooking. Thread the meat cubes on the wooden skewers. Grill the satés over charcoal or under a pre-heated grill, basting frequently with the sauce, until crisp, about 5 to 10 minutes.

Serve with peanut or tomato sauce. They are perfect as a starter for a barbecue, or as a main course with boiled rice and a green vegetable such as mangetout peas.

Heat scale 4

Curried Beef Crescents

THAILAND

Makes 24–36

These spicy beef crescents are somewhat similar to the *empanaditas* (little pies or turnovers) of Latin America. If you prefer, buy wuntun skins from a Chinese or Asian grocer and use them instead of making the pastry. Serve as an hors d'oeuvre, or a snack with drinks before dinner.

The filling

1 small onion, finely chopped
2 cloves garlic, finely chopped
40g/1½ oz butter
6 green chillies, skinned, seeds
    removed, chopped
1 tbsp grated fresh ginger root
450g/1 lb minced beef
½ tsp ground cumin
½ tsp ground coriander
½ tsp turmeric
2 tbsp lime juice
salt

The pastry

225g/8 oz lard or shortening
350g/12 oz flour
½ tsp salt
water

For the filling, sauté the onion and garlic in the butter until soft but not brown. Add the chillies and ginger and simmer for 5 minutes. Brown the beef in the mixture, stirring constantly. When the meat has browned, add the remaining ingredients. Remove from the heat.

For the pastry, cut the fat into the flour with a pastry blender, or two forks, or rub in, until the mixture is the consistency of coarse breadcrumbs. Add the salt and enough water to mix to a firm dough. Roll out to a 3-mm/⅛-in thickness and cut into 7.5-cm/3-in circles.

To assemble, place a teaspoon of the spiced beef filling in the centre of each circle of dough, or wuntun skin. Moisten the edges with water, fold the dough over, pressing the edges to seal, and pull the two ends towards the centre to form a crescent.

Place on ungreased baking sheets and bake at 190°C/375°F/Gas mark 5 for 25 minutes, or until the crusts are golden brown. Deep-fry if using wuntun skins.

Heat scale 2

Vietnamese Spicy Prawn Pork Salad

Needs advance preparation

Serves 4–6

A gourmet feast made from cold roast pork – among other things . . .

¼ tsp cayenne or 3 red chillies, finely
    chopped, or a few drops Tabasco
    sauce
2 cloves garlic, very finely chopped
¼ tsp ground coriander
2 tbsp vinegar
2 tbsp lemon juice
1 tsp sugar
salt and pepper
350g/¾ lb prawns or shrimps,
    cooked, and diced if large
225g/8 oz left-over cooked pork,
    diced
175g/6 oz rice vermicelli

Combine the cayenne, chilli or Tabasco, garlic, coriander, vinegar, lemon juice, sugar, salt and pepper in a bowl. Add the prawns or shrimps and pork and toss lightly until well coated. Allow to marinate for 1 hour before serving.

Bring the vermicelli to the boil in salted water. Remove from heat, cover and let stand for 5 minutes. Drain and allow to cool. Add the marinated seafood and meat to the noodles. Toss and serve.

Indonesian Chicken Soup, Vietnamese Spicy Prawn Pork Salad

Heat scale 8

Sambal

INDONESIA

Makes about 150ml/¹/₄ pt

Sambals are condiments, sauces, relishes and pastes with one common ingredient – hot chillies. The other ingredients may be plain or elaborate, but the sambals are always hot.

3 cloves garlic, minced
6–8 dried red hontaka (Japanese) chillies, crushed
3 tbsp peanut oil
¹/₂ tsp shrimp paste or dried shrimp, finely chopped
3 tbsp chopped spring onion (including green parts)
2 tbsp lime juice

Sauté the garlic and the chillies in the hot oil for 2 or 3 minutes. Stir the shrimp paste or dried shrimp into the mixture. Add the onion and lime juice and simmer the mixture until thickened. Cool to room temperature before serving.

Serve as an accompaniment to grilled meats, or as a sauce to dip satés in (page 83). Use sparingly!

Heat scale 8

Green Curry Paste

THAILAND

Makes about 150ml/¹/₄ pt

This is the Oriental counterpart of Latin America's Red Chilli Paste (page 118). It is the hottest of the hot Thai curries, due to the large number of small green serrano chillies traditionally used. This paste can be cooled down naturally, by reducing the amount of chilli or by adding coconut milk or cream (page 87). It will keep for a month or more in the refrigerator and though it may look like Italian *pesto*, don't confuse the two in your cooking or you'll be sorry!

10–12 serrano chillies, seeds removed, chopped or 5 fresh green chillies, chopped plus ¹/₂ tsp cayenne or Tabasco sauce
1 tsp chopped fresh ginger root
1 tsp coriander seeds
1 tsp caraway seeds
¹/₄ tsp ground cloves
1 tsp ground nutmeg
3 cloves garlic, chopped
2 tsp grated lemon rind
2 tbsp chopped spring onions
1 tsp shrimp paste or dried shrimp (from Oriental grocers)
3 tbsp vegetable oil

Combine all the ingredients in a blender or food processor and purée to a smooth paste.

Serve in sauces and combination dishes where a potent heat source is required. It may also be used as a condiment.

Coconut Milk and Cream

PACIFIC ISLANDS

The easiest way of making coconut milk is to buy 225g/8 oz blocks of creamed coconut. Dilute with milk or water as instructed on the package.

If you want to use a fresh coconut, grate the peeled flesh into a bowl and pour in about 450ml/¾ pint water that is just below boiling point. Leave to steep for about 1 hour, then strain off the coconut milk through a muslin-lined sieve.

If you have a blender or food processor, work the coconut flesh to a purée, then add the hot water and process until smooth. Leave to steep, then strain as above. Makes about 600ml/1 pint.

To make coconut milk from flaked coconut, steep the coconut in hot water. About 100g/4oz coconut makes 300ml/½ pint coconut milk.

To make coconut cream, dilute 100g/4 oz creamed coconut with 250ml/8 fl oz heated double cream. Steep and strain as above. Alternatively, use about 300ml/½ pint heated double cream to the grated flesh of 1 small coconut.

Note Take care when heating cream, or cooking with coconut milk or cream. Heat it slowly or it will curdle.

Burmese Beef

Heat scale 2

Needs advance preparation

Serves 4–6

3 tsp grated red chillies
4 tsp chopped fresh ginger root
1 large onion, chopped
3 cloves garlic, chopped
8 tbsp oil
1kg/2 lb best braising steak, cubed
2 tomatoes, peeled and chopped
250ml/8 fl oz water
2 tbsp soy sauce

Serve this beef dish over thin noodles with hard-boiled egg slices, shredded coconut and chopped mangoes.

Purée the chilli, ginger, onion and garlic to a paste and mix with 6 tablespoons of the oil. Add the beef and toss until well coated. Marinate the beef in the mixture for 4 hours in the refrigerator.

Brown the meat mixture in the remaining oil. Add the tomatoes, water and soy sauce. Cover and cook until the meat is tender, about 1 hour.

Overleaf: Beef Saté with tomato sauce, Green Curry Paste and Sambal

Heat scale 3

Spiced Curry

THAILAND

Serves 4–6

Thailand is known for its hot curries, but this is a relatively mild one. The cinnamon and brown sugar provide a hint of sweetness to complement the heat.

2 cloves garlic, minced
1 medium onion, chopped
4 tbsp oil
1kg/2 lb steak, cubed
3 tbsp Curry Powder (page 23)
450ml/³⁄4 pt beef stock
2 dried red chillies, whole
1 tbsp brown sugar
1 tsp cinnamon
150ml/¹⁄4 pt soured cream
chopped peanuts or cashew nuts

Sauté the garlic and onion in the hot oil until soft. Add the steak and brown on all sides. Add the curry powder and heat for 2 minutes. Add the stock, chillies, sugar and cinnamon. Bring to the boil, then cover and simmer until the beef is tender and there is about a cup of liquid left. Remove the chillies. Slowly stir in the soured cream. Garnish with the nuts and serve.

Serve with boiled rice and fruit such as chopped apples, bananas and raisins. Also good with fruit chutneys.

Heat scale 5

Sautéed Pork

CAMBODIA

Serves 6

For a quick and easy dinner serve this pork dish with stir-fried rice and vegetables like mangetout peas and bean sprouts.

4 dried red hontaka (Japanese)
  chillies, crumbled
900g/2 lb lean pork, cut in 2.5-cm/
  1-in cubes
3 medium onions, finely chopped
2 cloves garlic, very finely chopped
1 tbsp oil (peanut preferred)
3 tbsp light soy sauce
250ml/8 fl oz water
2 tbsp brown sugar
1 tbsp vinegar

Sauté the chillies, pork, onions and garlic in the oil for 10 minutes, stirring constantly. Add the remaining ingredients and simmer, stirring occasionally, until the pork is tender.

Preceding page: Fried Spiced Fish

Singapore Spare Ribs

Heat scale 3

Serves 6–8

The chillies provide the heat and the ginger an interesting pungency in these Oriental-flavoured ribs.

1–1.5kg/2–3 lb spare ribs, cut in 2- or 3-rib serving pieces
4 cloves garlic, halved
4 green chillies, skinned, seeds removed, chopped
2 tbsp peanut oil
175g/6 oz pineapple chunks
1 red or green pepper, seeds removed, sliced
250ml/8 fl oz pineapple juice
2 tbsp vinegar
5-cm/2-in piece fresh ginger root, peeled and chopped
2 tbsp brown sugar
1 tbsp dry sherry
1 tbsp dark soy sauce
2 tsp cornflour mixed with 2 tbsp water

Set the oven at 180°C/350°F/Gas mark 4.

Rub the ribs with the cut cloves of garlic and bake, uncovered, on a rack in the pre-heated oven for 1 hour.

Sauté the chillies in the oil for 2 minutes. Add the pineapple chunks and sauté for 3 more minutes. Add all the remaining ingredients except the cornflour and bring to the boil. Reduce the heat and simmer for 10 minutes.

Remove the ribs from the oven and pour off the fat. Baste the ribs with the sauce and cook for 1 hour more, basting frequently, until the ribs are crisp.

Remove the ribs and place the roasting tin over a medium heat. Add the remaining sauce, bring to the boil, and slowly stir in the cornflour mixture until the sauce thickens and becomes translucent. Pour the sauce over the ribs and serve.

Serve with plain boiled rice and Chinese leaves or spinach.

Marinated Pork

Heat scale 3

BURMA

Needs advance preparation

Serves 4–6

There are many versions of marinated pork in Burma. We have included our favourite and a variation.

3 tsp very finely chopped red chillies
3 tsp finely chopped fresh ginger root
1 medium onion, coarsely chopped
2 tbsp lime juice
2 tbsp oil
1 tbsp light soy sauce
2 tbsp water
salt to taste
450–575g/1–1½ lb boneless pork, cut in 2.5-cm/1-in cubes

Combine all the ingredients, except the pork, in a blender or food processor and purée until smooth. Marinate the pork in the mixture for 3 hours.

Thread the pork on skewers and grill over charcoal until the pork is crisp, basting frequently with the marinade.

Variation Substitute 3 tablespoons curry powder for the ginger, and honey for the oil, for a sweeter marinade.

Hawaiian Curried Chicken

Heat scale 2

Serves 4–6

Hawaii is at the crossroads of many cultures and this recipe reflects the variety that can be found in Pacific Island cookery.

2 tsp finely chopped fresh ginger root
1 small onion, chopped
25g/1 oz butter
2 tbsp Curry Powder (page 23)
450ml/¾ pt coconut milk (page 87)
1 tbsp flour mixed with 2 tbsp water
900g/2 lb cooked chicken, cut in cubes
50g/2 oz shredded coconut
8–10 pineapple chunks, drained

Sauté the ginger and onion in the butter until soft. Add the curry powder and heat for an additional 2 minutes. Slowly add the coconut milk, stirring constantly. Simmer over low heat for 30 minutes, being careful not to let it boil. Remove and strain.

Return the sauce to the heat and slowly stir in the flour and heat until slightly thickened. Add the chicken and simmer for 10 minutes, or until the chicken is heated. Top with the coconut and pineapple chunks and serve.

Malaysian Chicken

Heat scale 4

Serves 4–6

Once again peanuts crop up in combination with hot chillies.

4 dried red chillies, crumbled
1 large onion, finely chopped
2 cloves garlic, very finely chopped
3 tbsp peanut oil
1 tbsp brown sugar
1.5-kg/3-lb chicken, cut into pieces
4 tbsp light soy sauce
4 tbsp wine vinegar
2 tbsp water

Sauté the chillies, onion and garlic in the peanut oil until the onion is soft. Add the sugar and sauté until the onion turns brown. Add the chicken and fry until the chicken is uniformly browned.

Combine the remaining ingredients and add them to the chicken. Cover and simmer for 15 minutes. Remove the cover and cook over moderate heat for 30 minutes, or until the chicken is tender, basting occasionally with the sauce.

Curried Beef Crescents, Nasi Goreng

Heat scale 2

Curried Duck

PHILIPPINES

Serves 4–6

Curry is said to remove the fat, gamey taste of duck, as evidenced by this recipe.

1 oven-ready duck, cut in 5-cm/2-in
  pieces
2 tbsp oil
2 tbsp Curry Powder (page 23)
5-cm/2-in piece of fresh ginger root,
  peeled and minced
450ml/¾ pt water
2 tbsp tomato ketchup
2 tsp light soy sauce
4 spring onions, chopped (including
  green parts)

Sauté the duck pieces in the oil until browned. Pour off the fat. Mix the curry powder, ginger, water, ketchup and soy sauce together. Add the duck and simmer for 45 minutes or until the duck is tender. Garnish with the onions.

Serve over rice.

Heat scale 2

Malaysian Spiced Duck

Serves 6

Malaysians are very fond of curry dishes but seldom use a commercial curry powder. Individual spice pastes are prepared for each dish.

2 tsp ground ginger
1 tsp ground cumin
2 tsp ground coriander
1 large onion, finely chopped
2 cloves garlic, very finely chopped
150g/5 oz cashew nuts, ground
3 tsp ground dried red chilli
1 onion, thinly sliced and separated
  into rings
250ml/8 fl oz coconut cream
  (page 87)
salt
100g/4 oz fresh breadcrumbs
3 hard-boiled eggs, chopped
2.25-kg/5-lb oven-ready duck

Purée the ginger, cumin, coriander, chopped onion, garlic and cashews to a paste. Reserve 2 tablespoons of the spice paste and combine the rest with the chilli, sliced onion, three-quarters of the coconut cream, and the salt. Cook over a low heat for 15 minutes. Add the breadcrumbs and eggs. Stuff the duck with the mixture.

Mix the 2 reserved tablespoons of the spice paste with the rest of the coconut cream and rub the outside of the duck with the mixture. Roast the duck in an oven set at 180°C/350°F/Gas mark 4 until tender – about 1½ to 2 hours – basting frequently with any remaining spice paste and the drippings. Prick the skin of the duck frequently during cooking to allow the excess fat to drain away.

Fried Spiced Fish

THAILAND

Serves 4–6

A whole cooked fish makes an impressive entrée and this pungent example is no exception.

1–1.5kg/2–3 lb grey mullet or
  bream, cleaned but left whole
cornflour for dredging
oil for deep-frying
4 red chillies, seeds removed,
  crushed
5-cm/2-in piece ginger root, peeled
  and chopped
2 cloves garlic, very finely chopped
2 tbsp peanut oil
3 tbsp wine vinegar
6 tbsp water
2 tbsp light soy sauce
4 tbsp brown sugar
3 spring onions, chopped (including
  green parts)
2 tsp cornflour dissolved in 2 tbsp
  water

Make 4 or 5 deep incisions in each side of the fish and dredge in the cornflour. Heat the oil in a large frying pan until very hot. Gently lower the fish into the oil and fry until browned, about 5 to 10 minutes. Remove and drain.

Sauté the chillies, ginger and garlic in the peanut oil for 2 to 3 minutes. Add the remaining ingredients, except the cornflour, and bring to the boil. Reduce the heat and simmer for 5 minutes. Slowly stir in the cornflour until the sauce thickens and turns translucent. Pour the sauce over the fish and serve whole.

Serve accompanied by sliced fresh fruit or a chutney.

Indonesian Prawns

Serves 2–4

Coconut milk, ginger and chillies are a common combination in Indonesian cooking. This prawn dish could well be a part of a *rijsttafel*, which is an elaborate brunch or buffet lasting for hours.

3 tsp finely chopped red chilli
1 tsp grated fresh ginger root
1 clove garlic, finely chopped
2 small onions, finely chopped
2 tsp brown sugar
2 tsp lemon juice
2 tbsp oil
450g/1 lb uncooked prawns, peeled
  and de-veined
250ml/8 fl oz coconut milk
  (page 87)

Purée the first six ingredients in a blender to a smooth paste. Sauté the paste in hot oil for 5 minutes, stirring constantly. Add the prawns and sauté, stirring constantly, until the prawns are well coated. Slowly add the coconut milk, cover and simmer for 15 to 20 minutes.

Heat scale 6

Prawns in Green Curry Paste

THAILAND

Serves 4–6

The green colour is derived from the green chillies used in the paste. This is a relatively easy curry to prepare.

4 tbsp Green Curry Paste (page 86)
250ml/8 fl oz coconut milk
   (page 87)
900g/2 lb uncooked prawns, peeled
   and de-veined
small bunch spring onions, chopped
   (including green parts)

Simmer the green curry paste in half the coconut milk for 5 minutes. Add the prawns, stirring occasionally until they are cooked. Add the remaining coconut milk and simmer, uncovered, for an additional 10 minutes. Garnish with the onions.

Serve over rice.

Variation Cooked chicken may be substituted for the prawns.

Heat scale 5

Nasi Goreng

INDONESIA

Serves 4–6

Indonesia's version of fried rice can be made with one or more main ingredients – meat, chicken, or vegetables topped with chopped nuts.

225g/8 oz long-grain rice, rinsed well
450ml/³⁄4 pt chicken stock
3 tbsp oil (peanut preferred)
3 eggs, lightly beaten with
   1 tbsp water
1 large onion, finely chopped
3 cloves garlic, very finely chopped
2¹⁄2 tsp dried hot (hontaka or
   Japanese) chillies, crushed
3 tsp Curry Powder (page 23)
2–3 cooked chicken portions, cut in
   slices
100g/4 oz cooked prawns, chopped
2 tbsp soy sauce
4 tbsp cashews, chopped

Cook the rice in the chicken stock.

Heat 1 tablespoon of the oil in a pan until hot. Add the eggs and fry for 3 minutes each side. Remove this 'omelette' and cut into strips.

Sauté the onion and garlic in the rest of the oil until soft. Add the chillies and curry powder, and cook for 2 more minutes. Drain and stir in the cooked rice and sauté until the rice is brown. Add the chicken, prawns, soy sauce, most of the omelette strips and cook over a low heat, stirring occasionally, for 15 minutes or until thoroughly heated. Garnish with the chopped cashew nuts and remaining omelette strips.

Mexico

Mexico undoubtedly has the most sophisticated use of chillies of any of the world's fieriest cuisines, Literally hundreds of varieties grow in Mexico, and they are prepared and served in innumerable ways: fresh, dried, pickled, in sauces, soups, stews and with seafood, meat, poultry and vegetables.

Now that Mexican fare is becoming widely popular outside its country of origin, we are learning that there is more to it than the tortilla or taco (a fried tortilla), refried beans and a hot chilli-tomato sauce, though this has been the staple Mexican Indian diet since long before the Spanish invasion. Cheese, avocados, spices, chocolate, limes and tequila all play their part in the fish, meat and poultry dishes that follow.

Mexican dishes often use more than one type of chilli, blending them for flavour as well as for heat. Although it is simply not possible to find the same range of chillies outside Mexico, we have specified a particular variety where we feel it might be helpful. Do not feel that you cannot cook the dish without the requisite chilli – there has to be adjustment here. Use fresh or canned green chillies if you cannot find the long, tapering green jalapeño or the shorter, fatter green serrano – both fiery hot. And look for the dried red hontaka, or Japanese, chillies to use for the hottest dishes. Even then, do not despair; cayenne pepper or chilli powder will provide the necessary heat without masking the flavour of the other ingredients. If you feel inspired, however, make a study of the pasilla, ancho, mulato (black) and pequín chillies.

Heat scale 4

Chicken Corn Soup

Serves 4

Three staples of Mexican cuisine – chillies, chicken and corn – are combined in this simple soup.

1 small onion, chopped
25g/1 oz butter or margarine
4 green chillies, skinned, seeds removed, chopped
4 tbsp cooked diced potatoes
225g/8 oz cooked diced chicken
175g/6 oz cooked corn kernels
1 l/1¾ pt chicken stock
salt to taste

Sauté the onion in the butter until soft. Add all the remaining ingredients and simmer, covered, for 30 minutes.

Serve for lunch with sliced avocados and flour tortillas, or as the first course of a light dinner of cheese Enchiladas (page 112) and rice.

Variation Stir in 6 tablespoons double cream just before serving.

Molé Sauce

Heat scale 4

Makes about 1 l/1¾ pt

Pronounced '*mo*-lay', this subtle blend of chocolate with chilli is often called the 'National Dish of Mexico' when combined with turkey. It can be used in a number of ways.

4 dried red chilli pods, seeds
   removed
4 dried black (pasilla or mulato)
   chillies, seeds removed
1 medium onion, chopped
2 cloves garlic, chopped
2 medium tomatoes (red or green),
   peeled and chopped
2 tbsp sesame seeds
75g/3 oz almonds
½ corn tortilla (page 110) torn into
   pieces
50g/2 oz raisins
¼ tsp each of cloves, cinnamon and
   coriander
40g/1½ oz lard or shortening
250ml/8 fl oz chicken stock
25g/1 oz bitter chocolate (or more to
   taste)
salt to taste

Combine the chillies, onion, garlic, tomatoes, 1 tablespoon of the sesame seeds and the almonds. Add the tortilla pieces, raisins, cloves, cinnamon and coriander. Purée this mixture in a blender, a little at a time, until smooth.

Melt the lard in a frying pan and sauté the purée for 10 minutes, stirring frequently. Add the chicken stock, chocolate and salt and cook over a very low heat for 45 minutes. The sauce should be very thick. The remaining sesame seeds are used as a garnish.

Serve this classic sauce over turkey breast, garnished with the remaining sesame seeds. It is also excellent as an enchilada sauce over shredded chicken or turkey Enchiladas (page 112).

Salsa Borracha

Heat scale 7

Makes about 600ml/1 pt

Freely translated 'Salsa Borracha' means 'drunken sauce'; it gets its name from the tequila.

6–8 fresh green chillies, skinned,
   seeds removed
2 tbsp oil
1 medium onion, chopped
1 clove garlic, chopped
250ml/8 fl oz orange juice
3 tbsp tequila
salt to taste

Sauté the chillies in the oil for 10 minutes over a low heat and remove from the pan. Sauté the onion and garlic in the oil until soft.

Blend the chillies and orange juice in a blender until smooth. Add to the onion and cook for 10 minutes more. Add the tequila just before serving, being careful not to let it boil.

Serve this very versatile sauce as a barbecue sauce or a marinade for pork, lamb, chicken or beef.

Variation Use 175ml/6 fl oz orange and 3 tablespoons lemon or lime juice. Substitute white rum for the tequila. For a sweeter sauce, add 1–2 teaspoons honey. Substitute dried red chillies for the green chillies.

Guacamole

Avocado Salad

Makes up to 600ml/1 pt

There are many versions of this tasty dish and most contain chilli in some form. Recommended are fresh green chillies, but canned or fresh red, jalapeño or serrano chillies may be used.

3 fresh green chillies, skinned, seeds removed, finely chopped
1 tomato, finely chopped
3 ripe avocados, mashed
1 medium onion, finely chopped
¼ tsp garlic paste (or more)
pinch each of cumin and dried oregano (optional)
juice of 1 lemon
salt to taste

Combine all ingredients and mix well.

Serve over chopped lettuce as a salad, or as a dip with tortilla chips or corn chips. Use as a topping for Chimichangas (page 151) or Enchiladas (page 112).

Prawn-stuffed Avocados

Needs advance preparation

Serves 4 as a main course

From the vast coastal regions of Mexico comes this spicy prawn salad that makes a splendid lunch dish, or can be served in smaller portions as a starter or snack.

3–4 green chillies, skinned, seeds removed, chopped
1½ tbsp Red Chilli Sauce (page 146)
6 tbsp mayonnaise
3 tbsp finely chopped onion
1 clove garlic, very finely chopped
450g/1 lb cooked shelled prawns
2 avocados, halved just before serving

Mix together the chillies, Chilli Sauce, mayonnaise, onion and garlic. Add the prawns, toss until well coated, and marinate overnight in the refrigerator. When ready to serve, divide the prawn mixture evenly among the avocado halves.

Serve garnished with parsley or fresh coriander.

Carne Asada

Needs advance preparation

Serves 4–6

Carne Asada refers to meat that is roasted, grilled or barbecued. Our recipe calls for the meat to be marinated overnight before being cooked.

250ml/8 fl oz Green Chilli Sauce
   (page 146)
1 tsp dry mustard
1 tsp Worcestershire sauce
1 small onion, chopped
1 tbsp red wine
4 tbsp oil
2 tbsp sugar
2 tbsp lime juice
½ tsp salt
700g/1½ lb sirloin or rump steak,
   4-cm/1½ in thick

Combine all the ingredients except the steak and simmer for 15 minutes, then cool. Add the steak and marinate in the sauce overnight.

Remove the steak and reserve the marinade. Grill the steak and heat the marinade separately.

Serve the steak carved diagonally across the grain in thin strips, with the sauce on the side, accompanied by Green Rice (page 156).

Heat scale 4

Molé de Olla

Pot Stew

Serves 4

Molé means 'mixture' in Spanish, so the word crops up in recipes that have nothing to do with the traditional chocolate molé sauce. Here is a molé or stew that is as tasty as it is unusual.

700g/1½ lb braising steak, cubed
2 tbsp vegetable oil
4 or 5 green chillies, skinned, seeds
   removed, chopped
2 medium onions, chopped
1 clove garlic, chopped
½ tsp cinnamon
¼ tsp ground cloves
750ml/1¼ pt water
175g/6 oz raw corn kernels
100g/4 oz green beans
4 courgettes, sliced
salt to taste

Brown the meat in the oil. Purée the chillies, onions, garlic, cinnamon and cloves in 250ml/8 fl oz water. Combine the remaining water, the meat, corn and beans with the chilli mixture and simmer for 1 hour. Add the courgettes and cook the stew for 30 minutes more. Add more water if necessary, but the stew should be fairly thick.

Serve with corn bread or flour tortillas (page 111) and a green salad.

Molé de Olla, Guacamole, Chilli Corn Bread

Heat scale 5

Carnero Adobo

Serves 6–8

Beef or pork can be substituted for the lamb in this dish. *Adobo* relates to the thick sauce or paste of chillies, vinegar and spices.

900g/2 lb boneless lamb, cut into 2.5-cm/1-in cubes
2 cloves garlic, very finely chopped or crushed
2 medium onions, chopped
3–4 sprigs fresh coriander
salt to taste
water (see method)
6 dried red chillies
¼ tsp ground cumin
½ tsp dried oregano
2 tbsp red wine vinegar
40g/1½ oz lard or shortening

Place the lamb in a heavy saucepan or casserole with half the garlic and half the onion, the coriander, salt, and enough water to barely cover. Bring to the boil, reduce the heat, cover and simmer until the meat is tender, about 1½ hours. Remove the lamb, and strain and reserve the stock.

Place the chillies, remaining onion and garlic, cumin, oregano, vinegar and a little more salt in a blender or food processor and purée to a fairly smooth paste.

Sauté the chilli mixture in the lard, stirring constantly, for 5 minutes. Thin the mixture with about 300ml/½ pint of the reserved lamb stock until it is the consistency of a medium white sauce. Add the lamb to the sauce and simmer over low heat for 20 minutes.

Heat scale 4

Javelina Roast

Serves 6–8

The pork in this pre-Columbian recipe is that of the javelina, or peccary, which was a staple in Mexico before the advent of the domesticated pig. We have substituted a pork roast for the wild pig.

2 cloves garlic, finely chopped
½ tsp dried oregano
½ tsp dried sage
2 tsp salt
2kg/4½ lb joint of pork
3 tbsp onion, finely chopped
4 tbsp flour
6 tbsp Red Chilli Sauce (page 146)
6 tbsp tomato purée
50g/2 oz raisins (optional)
water (see method)

Mix the garlic, oregano, sage and salt together and rub the mixture into the meat. Place the meat, fat side up, in a roasting tin and roast at 180°C/350°F/Gas mark 4 for 2 hours. Remove the meat and keep warm.

Pour the drippings into a frying pan, add the onion and sauté until the onion is transparent. Thicken the drippings with the flour and add the Chilli Sauce, tomato purée and raisins. Add enough water to achieve the desired consistency and simmer for 10 minutes.

Return the meat to the tin, baste with the sauce and roast for 30 minutes more, basting 2 or 3 times with the sauce.

Serve sliced and covered with the sauce, accompanied by roast potatoes or green rice.

Chicken with Lime Sauce

Serves 4

Don't let the long list of ingredients put you off. This dish requires some work, but it is well worth the extra effort.

4 boneless chicken breasts
3 tbsp flour, plus extra for dredging the chicken
100g/4 oz butter
6 tbsp tequila
4 green chillies, skinned, seeds removed, chopped
grated rind and juice of 2 large limes
2 cloves garlic, crushed
250ml/8 fl oz chicken stock
150ml/¼ pt soured cream
150ml/¼ pt double cream
2 tsp sugar
salt and white pepper to taste
75g/3 oz Parmesan cheese, grated

Dredge the chicken in flour and quickly brown in about 50g/2 oz of the butter. Pour half the tequila over the chicken and set alight. When the flame dies down, remove the chicken and set aside.

Add the remaining butter to the pan used to brown the chicken and heat. Slowly add the chillies, lime rind and garlic and cook for 4 minutes. Add the 3 tablespoons flour, the rest of the tequila, and the chicken stock. Slowly bring the mixture to the boil, stirring constantly. Immediately reduce the heat and simmer for 5 minutes. Gently stir the soured cream and double cream into the sauce and add the lime juice and sugar.

Return the chicken to the pan, cover with the sauce and simmer until tender, about 30 minutes. Adjust the seasoning.

When done, place the chicken in a serving dish, cover with the sauce, and top with the Parmesan cheese. Place under the grill only long enough to brown the cheese.

Serve with a salad and plain vegetables.

Pollo Pasilla

Chicken with Pasilla Chillies

The sweetness of the honey is cut by the heat of the chillies and the sourness of the lemon or lime juice.

Serves 4

6–8 pasilla or dried red chillies, seeds removed
450ml/¾ pt hot water
6 chicken thighs or 4 chicken breasts
100g/4 oz butter
1 onion, finely chopped
6 tbsp honey
juice of 2 lemons or limes

Soak the chillies in the hot water.

Brown the chicken in half the butter, turning frequently, and remove. Sauté the onion in the remaining butter until browned.

Purée the chillies in the water with the honey and lemon or lime juice until smooth. Add the mixture to the browned onions and cook over low heat for 10 minutes.

Place the chicken in a shallow dish, baste with the sauce, and bake at 180°C/350°F/Gas mark 4 for 30 minutes, or until the chicken is done, basting frequently with the sauce.

Serve garnished with orange slices, and with plain rice.

Heat scale 3

Fish in Chilli Almond Sauce

Serves 4–6

With over 5000 miles of coastline and lakes, it is easy to see why fish dishes are popular in Mexico. This one is unusual – and delicious.

450ml/¾ pt water or court bouillon
6 plaice or haddock fillets
4 serrano or jalapeño chillies, or 4 fresh green chillies, chopped
1 clove garlic
1 slice white bread, crusts removed
75g/3 oz blanched almonds
small bunch of fresh coriander or parsley, chopped
salt and pepper to taste

Bring the water or bouillon to the boil and add the fish fillets. Reduce the heat, cover and simmer until the fish flakes easily but does not fall apart, about 8 to 10 minutes. Remove the fish and reserve the bouillon.

Combine the chillies, garlic, bread, almonds, coriander or parsley and reserved bouillon in a blender and purée until smooth. Transfer the mixture to a pan and simmer until the sauce thickens. Pour the sauce over the fish and serve.

Serve the fish arranged on a bed of rice, pour the sauce over the top, and garnish with extra sliced almonds. Serve with baked yams for colour contrast.

Heat scale 4

Guatemalan Red Mullet

Serves 6

At first the combination of hot chillies with fish seems unusual, but similar dishes appear in cuisines all over the world. Virtually any fresh or canned chillies will work in this well-known Mexican dish.

6 red mullet
4 tbsp lime or lemon juice
flour seasoned with a little dried thyme, for coating fish
2–3 tbsp olive oil
1 medium onion, chopped
2 cloves garlic, crushed or very finely chopped
3 tomatoes, peeled and chopped
5 green chillies, chopped
3 tbsp tomato purée
¼ tsp cinnamon
¼ tsp ground cloves
250ml/8 fl oz water
stuffed green olives, sliced

Rub the fish with the lime or lemon juice and lightly coat with seasoned flour. Sauté the fish on both sides in olive oil until golden brown. Remove, set aside, and keep warm.

Sauté the onion and garlic in the oil until soft. Add all the remaining ingredients, except the fish, and simmer for 20 minutes. Place the fish in a large pan, cover with the sauce, and heat. Garnish with the sliced green olives and serve.

Serve with rice and green beans.

Fish in Chilli Almond Sauce, Chicken Corn Soup, Spicy Green Beans

Huevos con Chorizo

Heat scale 4

Eggs with Hot Sausage

Serves 4

Chorizos are very hot, spicy Spanish sausages that are made from beef or pork or a combination of both. They are seasoned with garlic, cayenne and chilli powder.

1 onion, finely chopped
15g/½ oz butter
1 clove garlic, crushed
3 green chillies, skinned, seeds removed, chopped
2 small chorizo or other spiced sausages, skinned and chopped
3 tomatoes, peeled and chopped
pinch of sugar
salt and pepper to taste
6 eggs, lightly beaten

Sauté the onion in the butter until soft. Add the garlic, chillies and sausages and continue cooking for 5 minutes. Add the tomatoes, sugar, salt and pepper and cook for 5 minutes more. Slowly stir in the eggs and cook until the eggs are set.

Serve with flour tortillas, fresh fruit compote and Mexican hot chocolate for a Sunday breakfast with a difference.

Huevos Rancheros

Heat scale 6

Ranch-style Eggs

Serves 2–4

There are many variations of this popular dish, and we have included this easy favourite of ours.

450ml/¾ pt Green or Red Chilli Sauce (page 146)
4 eggs
4 corn tortillas (page 110)
oil for frying
3 fresh green or red chillies, skinned, seeds removed, chopped
50g/2 oz Cheddar cheese, grated

Heat the Chilli Sauce in a shallow frying pan. Carefully slip the eggs into the hot sauce and poach to the desired firmness.

Fry each tortilla in hot oil only for a few seconds until soft, then drain. Place the eggs and sauce on the tortillas. Mound extra sauce around the edges and sprinkle the chopped chillies over the sauce. Top with the grated cheese and serve immediately.

Serve with Potatoes with Red Chilli (page 111) and flour tortillas and garnish the plate with avocado slices.

Arroz con Queso

Heat scale 3

Serves 4

Plain rice is transformed into a savoury side dish by the addition of chillies and cheese.

4 green chillies, skinned, seeds
    removed, diced
250ml/8 fl oz soured cream
225g/8 oz rice, cooked
100g/4 oz Cheddar cheese, grated

Combine the green chillies and soured cream in a bowl. Add the cooked rice and mix well. Pour this mixture into a greased baking tin and top with the grated cheese. Bake at 180°C/350°F/Gas mark 4 for 15 to 20 minutes, or until thoroughly heated and the cheese has melted.

Serve with plain fish, poultry or meat.

Elote con Crema

Heat scale 4

Serves 4–6

Translated from the Spanish, *Elote con Crema* means 'Corn with Cream'.

1 small onion, chopped
1 clove garlic, finely chopped
25g/1 oz butter
4–5 fresh green chillies, skinned,
    seeds removed, chopped
450g/1 lb corn kernels
salt and pepper to taste
50g/2 oz Cheddar cheese, cut into
    small cubes
soured cream for garnishing

Sauté the onion and garlic in the butter until soft. Add the chillies and cook for an additional 8 to 10 minutes. Stir in the corn, salt and pepper and transfer the mixture to a baking dish. Add the cheese cubes to the casserole and bake at 180°C/350°F/Gas mark 4 for 40 minutes. Top with the soured cream before serving.

Serve either as an extra vegetable with meat, or instead of potatoes or rice.

Variations Add sliced courgettes and cooked peeled potatoes.

Spicy Green Beans

Heat scale 4

Serves 4

These beans go particularly well with cheese dishes or cooked meats, but will add colour and heat to any meal.

1 medium onion, chopped
1 clove garlic, chopped
1 tbsp oil or lard
3–4 green chillies, skinned, seeds
    removed, chopped
450g/1 lb green beans
2 tomatoes, peeled and chopped
250ml/8 fl oz water
salt to taste

Sauté the onion and garlic in the oil until soft. Add the chillies and fry for 2 or 3 more minutes. Add the remaining ingredients, bring to the boil, reduce the heat, and simmer until the beans are done.

Baked Carrots

Heat scale 4

Serves 4

Jalapeños (small, hot green Mexican chillies) more often appear in uncooked dishes, but this unusual vegetable recipe shows their versatility. If you cannot find jalapeños use fresh chillies instead.

450g/1 lb carrots, cut in thin rounds
2 jalapeño chillies, sliced in rings, or
  fresh green chillies, sliced
6 tbsp water
salt to taste
25g/1 oz butter or margarine
¼ tsp cinnamon

Place the carrots and chillies in a baking dish. Add the water, salt to taste, and dot with the butter and cinnamon. Bake, covered, in a 180°C/350°F/Gas mark 4 oven until done, about 1 hour.

Frijoles Refritos

Refried Beans

Needs advance preparation

Serves 4–6

2 large (439g/15oz) cans red kidney
  beans
2 cloves garlic, crushed
2 tsp salt
1–2 tsp sugar
3 tbsp oil or 50g/2 oz lard

Drain the beans and put in a saucepan. Over low heat stir in the garlic, salt and sugar. Mash. Heat the oil or lard in a frying pan, add the beans and mix to a smooth, heavy paste. The beans can then be refried after the first serving, and they get better in flavour with each frying. If serving as an accompaniment, they should be about the consistency of mashed potatoes; if serving over tortillas, they should be more moist, like porridge. If refrying for a second time, add a little water first to adjust the consistency.

Heat 2 tablespoons oil or 25g/1 oz lard in a frying pan and add the mashed beans a little at a time, stirring and turning as they cook to prevent the beans from sticking and to help them to reheat evenly. Cook for 10–15 minutes over low heat, adding extra oil or lard as required.

Arroz con Queso, Baked Carrots, Chicken with Lime Sauce

Frijoles Para Sopear

Heat scale 4

Makes up to 750ml/1¼ pt

Bean Dip
This party dip is best served warm.

450g/1 lb Refried Beans (page 108)
4 green chillies, skinned, seeds removed, chopped
125ml/4 fl oz Green Chilli Sauce (page 146)
1 small onion, chopped
100g/4 oz Cheddar cheese, grated
salt to taste

In a saucepan, heat the beans until very hot. Add all the other ingredients and stir until the cheese melts. Add water, if necessary, to thin to the desired consistency for dipping.

Serve in a chafing dish or fondue pot as an hors d'oeuvre with corn or tortilla chips.

Corn Tortillas

Makes about 12

Some people say that it is almost impossible to make a creditable tortilla without a special tortilla press to get them wafer-thin, but it is possible – with a little practice – to roll them between sheets of cling film. Each tortilla should be about 15-cm/6-in in diameter, or larger – depending on the size of your frying pan – and about 3mm/⅛ in thick. A griddle pan is perfect for cooking tortillas.

275g/10 oz masa harina (fine maize flour)
pinch of salt
350ml/12 fl oz lukewarm water

Put the cornmeal flour in a bowl with the salt. Gradually work in the water to make a smooth, soft dough. Knead it as you would bread dough for up to 10 minutes by hand, 4–5 minutes with an electric mixer, or in a food processor, until a small ball of dough does not start to dissolve when placed in a small bowl of cold water.

Divide the dough into 12 pieces, roll each into a small ball and leave to stand for about 1 hour.

Place each dough ball between 2 sheets of cling film and roll out to a 15-cm/6-in circle. Heat a large, heavy-based frying pan until a few drops of cold water scatter and evaporate when sprinkled on the surface. Add a tortilla, cook for about 1 minute, until gold speckles start to appear on the top. Turn carefully and fry on the other side for 1–1½ minutes. Wrap in a warm cloth while frying the rest.

The tortillas are now ready for filling, or serving as accompaniments.

Tortillas will freeze well, and can be reheated from frozen.

Flour Tortillas

Makes about 18

These come from the northern part of Mexico and are usually larger than the Corn Tortillas (see previous recipe). It is said they were first made by the Spanish settlers, who cooked their own food, using Indian methods. These are delicious eaten hot with butter and salt, or spread with Guacamole (page 99) or a chilli sauce, then rolled round a cooked meat or cheese filling.

450g/1 lb plain flour
1 tbsp salt
75g/3 oz lard or vegetable shortening
about 300ml/½ pt lukewarm water

Sift the flour into a bowl with the salt and rub in the lard or shortening until the mixture resembles fine breadcrumbs. Gradually add the warm water and mix to a smooth dough. Knead on a well-floured board until the dough is no longer sticky, but fairly stiff without being hard.

Divide into walnut-size pieces and keep them covered with a warm damp cloth while working. One by one, roll them out as thin as possible, to a round about 23cm/9 in in diameter.

Heat a heavy-based frying pan until a few drops of cold water scatter and evaporate when sprinkled on the surface. Use a rolling pin, if necessary, to transfer each tortilla to the pan, and cook, one by one, for 30 seconds on one side, then turn and cook on the other side for up to 1 minute.

Stack them in a warm cloth as they are cooked, and eat while hot.

Note These also freeze well, between sheets of cling film or greaseproof paper. Reheat before serving and serve hot.

Heat scale 4

Enchiladas

Serves 4

Enchiladas are one of the most popular of all Mexican dishes and also one of the most 'adapted'. Those served in restaurant chains are made as bland as possible so as not to offend the meat-and-potatoes palate. The Enchiladas here are from traditional recipes served in Chihuahua. They may be served flat, with the stuffing between each layer of tortilla, or they may be rolled with the stuffing inside.

12 corn tortillas (page 110)
6 tbsp oil
350g/12 oz cooked minced meat
  (beef, chicken or pork)
225g/8 oz Cheddar cheese, grated
1 large onion, finely chopped
750ml/1¼ pt Red or Green Chilli
  Sauce (page 146)
shredded lettuce and chopped
  tomato for garnish

Fry each tortilla in hot oil for a few seconds until it is soft. Do not overcook or they will turn crisp. Drain on paper towels. Add the filling to the tortillas:

Rolled Enchiladas

Place some of the meat, cheese and onion on a tortilla and roll it up. Place three rolled Enchiladas on a heatproof plate, cover with Chilli Sauce, and sprinkle them with more cheese and onion.

Stacked Enchiladas

Place the meat, cheese and onion and a little sauce between layers of tortillas on a heatproof plate. Cover with Chilli Sauce, and sprinkle with cheese and onion.

Heat the enchilada plates in an oven or under a grill until the cheese just begins to brown.

Serve garnished with shredded lettuce and chopped tomatoes, or smothered with Guacamole (page 99) and garnished with soured cream. Often, Enchiladas are served with a fried egg on top. They go well with rice and beans.

Variations Enchilada casseroles are made from large numbers of rolled Enchiladas stacked in a casserole dish, baked in a chilli sauce, and topped with cheese. Bake for 1 hour at 180°C/350°F/Gas mark 4. For a dessert Enchilada, slice half a banana lengthways and fry in butter. Roll each section of banana in a tortilla, cover with Molé sauce (page 98) and bake at 180°C/350°F/Gas mark 4 for 15 minutes.

Enchiladas, Molé Sauce, Frijoles Para Sopear

Latin America

The diverse cuisines of Central and South America resulted from a collision of cultures. Indigenous Indians and Africans brought as slaves interacted with the French, English, Portuguese, Spanish, Dutch, German and Chinese settlers, producing amalgams of cuisines that persist to this day.

As might be expected in the land where these fiery fruits originated, chillies are the most important hot ingredient in Latin American dishes. Ginger, horseradish, coconut milk and mustard are also found in the dishes that follow, reflecting the rich mixture of cultures that inspired them. The combination of seafood and chillies is popular in Central America, along the Caribbean coast of South America, and in Peru and Chile, which gives us some of the world's hottest sauces. In addition to hot seafood dishes, Brazil enjoys the chilli-peanut combination, reflecting a strong African influence. On the whole the cuisine of Central America most resembles that of western and southern Mexico, and the cooking of South America depends less on sauces than on dishes in which the smaller, hotter chillies are added to meat and vegetables more for heat than flavour.

Chicken and Marrow Soup with Chilli Sauce

Heat scale 4

BOLIVIA

Serves 6–8

Hearty soups are common in South America. Serving the sauce on the side allows the individual to adjust the heat to their taste.

900g/2-lb oven-ready chicken, cut in
   pieces
1 medium onion, coarsely chopped
1.25 l/2¼ pt water
salt and pepper to taste
450g/1 lb marrow or pumpkin,
   peeled and cut into 2.5-cm/1-in
   cubes
⅛ tsp turmeric
250ml/8 fl oz Chilean Hot Sauce
   (page 119)

Put the chicken and onion in a pan with the water. Bring to the boil, adding salt and pepper to taste. Skim off any foam that forms. Reduce the heat and simmer until the chicken is tender but not falling off the bones. Remove the chicken and cut the meat off the bones, then chop.

Add the marrow or pumpkin and turmeric to the chicken stock and cook, covered, until the vegetable is tender, about 20 minutes.

114

Return the chicken to the pan and simmer until thoroughly heated. Heat the hot sauce in a small pan and pour into a serving bowl.

Serve the soup and sauce to each individual in separate bowls. The sauce is added to the soup until the desired pungency is obtained.

Bahia Peanut Soup

Heat scale 5

BRAZIL

Serves 4

The West African influence is strong in the cooking of Brazil, particularly in the Bahia area. This dish very definitely has an African flavour – note the combination of hot chillies and peanuts. We suggest you experiment with the quantity of dried shrimp, which are obtainable at Oriental or West Indian grocers. You may find that 200g/7 oz is enough initially.

1 tsp paprika
175g/6 oz okra, cut in small pieces
1 onion, chopped
salt to taste
1 l/1¾ pt water
450g/1 lb dried shrimps, shelled or to taste
25g/1 oz flour
175g/6 oz roasted cashew nuts
6 tbsp peanut butter
3 dried red hontaka (Japanese) chillies
1 tsp ground ginger

Place the paprika, okra, onion, salt and water in a pan and bring to the boil. Reduce the heat and cook until the okra is tender.

Purée the dried shrimps almost to a powder in a blender or processor. Mix with the flour and cashews until thoroughly blended. Thin the peanut butter to a thick paste with a little water. Mix the chillies, ginger, shrimp and peanut butter and heat slowly. Stir the peanut butter mixture into the okra. Bring to the boil and cook for 15 minutes, stirring constantly.

Ceviche

Heat scale 4

PERU

Needs advance preparation
Serves 6

There are similar raw fish dishes found in many countries throughout the world: Peru, Mexico, Ghana, Japan and Spain, to name a few. The lemon or lime juice 'cooks' the fish so it does not taste raw. Because of the high citric acid content of this dish, always use a ceramic or glass bowl – never a metal one.

700–900g/1½–2 lb firm-fleshed
   white fish (haddock, hake, cod)
450ml/¾ pt lime or lemon juice,
   fresh preferred
4–5 fresh green chillies, skinned,
   seeds removed, chopped
1 onion, sliced and separated into
   rings
6 tbsp olive oil
1 tbsp white vinegar
2 cloves garlic, chopped
3 tbsp chopped fresh parsley
¼ tsp dried oregano
salt and pepper to taste
4 canned pimentos, drained and cut
   into strips

Cover the fish with the lime or lemon juice and refrigerate for 6 hours, turning occasionally, until the fish loses its translucency and turns opaque. Drain and reserve the marinade.

Combine all the remaining ingredients except the pimento and add the marinade. Toss the fish in the combined marinade until well coated and then marinate for 2 more hours. Garnish with the pimento to serve.

Serve as a salad over lettuce. In Peru it is traditionally served as a starter.

Variations Substitute sliced scallops, shelled prawns or lobster for the white fish.

Heat scale 4

Brazilian Marinated Prawns

Needs advance preparation

Serves 4–6

This seafood delicacy combines chilli, mustard and horseradish in one recipe.

4 small hot red chillies, crushed
2 tsp Horseradish Sauce (page 27)
2 tbsp made mustard
6 tbsp peanut oil
4 tbsp white vinegar
juice of 1 lemon or lime
450g/1 lb cooked prawns, peeled
1 medium onion, sliced into rings
   and separated
fresh coriander or parsley, chopped

Combine the chillies, horseradish, mustard, oil, vinegar and lemon or lime juice and mix well. Add the prawns and onion rings and toss gently to cover the seafood. Marinate in the refrigerator for 8 hours, turning occasionally. Drain the prawns and onion before serving. Garnish with coriander or parsley.

Serve on a bed of lettuce as a salad or starter.

Variations Substitute scallops or firm-fleshed white fish.

Bolivian Baked Corn, Chilean Hot Sauce, Ecuadorean Pork Roast

Empanaditas

ARGENTINA

Makes 24

Variations on these spicy Spanish-style turnovers are found throughout Latin America, Mexico and the American South-west. There are an infinite number of combinations of fillings that can be used, so experiment with your own.

The filling
2 medium onions, finely chopped
1 tbsp oil
6 tbsp water
225g/8 oz sirloin steak, roughly chopped
3 tbsp raisins
1 tsp Red Chilli Paste (page 118) or ½ tsp cayenne or 1 tsp Tabasco sauce
¼ tsp ground cumin
½ tsp salt
2 hard-boiled eggs, sliced

The pastry
275g/10 oz flour
1 tsp salt
100g/4 oz lard or shortening
6 tbsp water

For the filling, combine the onions, oil and water in a frying pan and boil the mixture until the water has evaporated. Add the steak and brown on all sides. Add the raisins, chilli paste or cayenne, cumin and salt. Remove from the heat and set aside. (Add Tabasco now, if using.)

For the pastry, combine the flour, salt and lard or shortening and mix thoroughly with a pastry blender until the mixture has the texture of coarse crumbs. Add enough water to mix until the dough can be gathered into a compact ball. Roll out the dough to between 3–5 mm/⅛–¼ in thick. Cut the dough into 13-cm/5-in diameter circles.

To assemble the Empanaditas, place about 1½ tablespoons of filling in the centre of each circle of dough and top with an egg slice. Moisten the edges of the dough and fold them together to form a crescent. Press or crimp the edges firmly together to seal. Bake on an ungreased baking sheet for 20 minutes at 200°C/400°F/Gas mark 6, or until the pastry is cooked and browned.

Serve traditionally, as a hot hors d'oeuvre.

Variation Replace 1 tablespoon of the water with 1 tablespoon lime or lemon juice when making the pastry. Ready-made puff pastry can also be used.

Red Chilli Paste

CHILE and PERU

Makes about 300ml/½ pt

In South America this paste is often used in place of fresh chillies. A word of caution – this is an extremely hot paste, so use it sparingly! Pickled hot peppers from the Caribbean can be drained and used.

50g/2 oz hontaka (Japanese) hot chillies, seeds removed, or dried hot red chillies for a less pungent paste

Pour the boiling water over the chillies and let stand for 20 minutes or until the chillies are soft. Drain the chillies and combine with all the other ingredients. Place the mixture in a blender and purée until smooth.

250ml/8 fl oz boiling water
2 cloves garlic, finely chopped
250ml/8 fl oz chicken stock
6 tbsp oil

Serve as an accompaniment to grilled or roast meat, or with poultry. Place in a small bowl and allow guests to use as much as they dare. It can also be used in sauces and other dishes when a heat source is required.

Chilean Hot Sauce

Heat scale 4

Needs advance preparation

Makes about 300ml/½ pt

Of course, the number of chillies used will determine the heat scale of this sauce, so use as many as you dare.

1 tbsp red wine vinegar
2 tbsp oil
6 tbsp water
4 fresh green chillies, skinned, seeds removed, finely chopped or 1½ tbsp Red Chilli Paste (page 118)
1 medium onion, finely chopped
2 cloves garlic, finely chopped
3 tbsp chopped fresh coriander or parsley
salt to taste

Beat the vinegar, oil and water together until combined. Add the remaining ingredients and allow to sit for 3 or 4 hours at room temperature.

Serve with grilled meat, fish or poultry.

Variation Use red chillies in place of the green.

Vinegar Barbecue Sauce

Heat scale 8

ARGENTINA

This very hot sauce appears at barbecue roasts in cattle country – the Pampas. It is not designed for basting but to be added to the meat at the table.

Needs advance preparation

Makes about 250ml/8 fl oz

¾ tbsp dried hot (Japanese) chillies, crushed
175ml/6 fl oz red wine vinegar
3 tbsp peanut oil
3 cloves garlic, minced
¾ tsp dried oregano
salt and freshly ground pepper

Combine all the ingredients and allow to sit for at least 24 hours to blend all the flavours.

Serve brushed over shish kebabs or grilled steaks.

Heat scale 6

Matahambre

ARGENTINA

The title of this dish translates in varied ways as 'jungle hunger' or 'starving to death'. It is a hearty dish that varies in heat according to the cook. Matahambre is most often served hot, but is also delicious cold.

Needs advance preparation

Serves 6

6 tbsp beer
6 tbsp vinegar
3 tbsp oil
1 medium onion, chopped
2 cloves garlic, finely chopped
1 bay leaf
salt and pepper to taste
900g/2 lb sirloin steak, in one piece
6 fresh green chillies, skinned, seeds
    removed, finely chopped
2 potatoes, sliced into strips
2 carrots, thinly sliced lengthways
4 slices bacon, rinds removed

Mix the beer, vinegar, oil, half the onion and garlic, bay leaf, salt and pepper together. Marinate the steak in the mixture for 3 hours.

Remove the steak, reserving the marinade, and flatten the meat with a rolling pin. Spread the chillies, then the potatoes, carrots and bacon over the meat. Roll up the steak, taking care to turn the edges in so the stuffing does not fall out. Tie the roll with string to hold it together.

Place the rolled steak in a pan with half the remaining marinade and enough water to come up to the top of the meat. Add the remaining onion and garlic. Cover, and simmer for 2½ hours.

Serve the roll cut into slices with a little of the cooking juices spooned over each slice, accompanied by oven-browned potatoes and glazed carrots.

Heat scale 3

Churrasco

BRAZIL

A *churrasco*, or barbecue, is common in the southern parts of Brazil, where large cattle ranches are located. The barbecue feast can be a single main dish, or a traditional Churrasco. The latter is a variety of meats and sausages skewered on large 'swords' that are brought to the table.

Needs advance preparation

Serves 4–6

4 dried red chillies, stems and seeds
    removed, crushed
250ml/8 fl oz lemon juice
1 large onion, chopped
6 tbsp chopped fresh coriander or
    parsley
2 tsp salt
900g/2 lb rump steak
1 tsp cornflour mixed with 1 tbsp
    water

Combine all the ingredients and marinate the steak overnight. Remove the steak and grill or barbecue until cooked to taste. Make a sauce by heating and thickening the marinade with the cornflour mixture.

Serve the sauce spooned over the steak. In Brazil a Churrasco would be served with vegetables such as chopped greens, toasted manioc and black beans, and accompanied by fresh orange slices.

Ecuadorean Pork Roast

Heat scale 3

Needs advance preparation

Serves 4–6

This spiced roast is best served sliced and arranged on a serving dish, and then topped with the gravy. Serve with boiled potatoes and parslied, buttered carrots or minted green peas. Accompany with a bowl of Chilean Hot Sauce (page 119).

1½ tbsp crushed red chillies
4 cloves garlic
¼ tsp saffron mixed with 3 tbsp hot water
½ tsp cumin seeds
½ tsp dried marjoram
1 tsp salt
1 tsp freshly ground pepper
2-kg/4-lb pork loin
6 tbsp dry white wine
3 tbsp red wine vinegar
2 medium onions, finely chopped
2 tbsp flour mixed with 2 tbsp water

Make a paste of the chillies, garlic, saffron, cumin, marjoram, salt and pepper. Rub the paste into the pork roast and marinate overnight in the refrigerator.

Set the oven to 220°C/425°F/Gas mark 7 about 30 minutes before cooking.

Place the meat in a roasting tin and place in the pre-heated oven. Reduce the heat to 180°C/350°F/Gas mark 4, and cook for 2 hours or until the meat is done. Baste frequently with the drippings.

When done, remove the roast and skim the fat from the drippings. Add the wine, vinegar and onion to the drippings, heat, and thicken the gravy with the flour mixture.

Orange Spiced Pork Chops

Heat scale 4

COLUMBIA

Serves 4

This dish resembles some Oriental sweet-and-sour recipes. The heat of the chillies is tempered by the sweetness and acidity of the oranges.

1 small onion, sliced and separated into rings
25g/1 oz butter
4 pork loin chops
1 tbsp grated orange rind
6 tbsp orange juice
6 tbsp chicken stock
6 tbsp Chilean Hot Sauce (page 119)
2 tsp cornflour mixed with 1 tbsp water

Sauté the onion in the butter until soft. Remove from the pan. Brown the pork chops in the pan on both sides, and top with the onion.

Mix together the orange rind, orange juice, stock and hot sauce. Pour the sauce over the chops and simmer until the chops are tender, about 15 minutes. Remove the chops. Thicken the sauce with the cornflour mixture.

Serve the chops with the onion rings, topped with the thickened sauce and accompanied by a green vegetable and roast or baked potatoes.

Bolivian Stuffed Chicken

Serves 4

An exotic chicken variation that makes an excellent main course for a festive occasion. For extra heat, serve accompanied by Salsa Borracha (page 98).

2-kg/4-lb oven-ready chicken
3 cloves garlic, halved
225g/8 oz minced pork
4 tsp chilli powder
50g/2 oz cooked rice
1 small onion, chopped
3 tbsp tomato sauce
75g/3 oz raisins
75g/3 oz toasted almonds, chopped
25g/1 oz butter

Rub the chicken inside and out with the cut garlic. Mix together the remaining ingredients except the butter and stuff the chicken with the mixture. Dot the chicken with butter and roast in an oven set at 180°C/350°F/Gas mark 4 for 2 hours or until done. Baste frequently with the drippings.

Peruvian Chicken in Nut Sauce

Serves 4–6

In this delicious dish, the walnut sauce conceals a powerful heat.

2-kg/4-1lb oven-ready chicken,
    quartered
about 900ml/1½ pt chicken stock
175g/6 oz fresh breadcrumbs
450ml/¾ pt milk
1 medium onion, finely chopped
3 cloves garlic, finely chopped
4 tbsp oil
3 dried red hontaka (Japanese)
    chillies, crushed, or 3 tbsp Red
    Chilli Paste (page 118)
100g/4 oz walnuts, ground
salt and pepper to taste
25g/1 oz crumbled white cheese
    (Caerphilly or white Cheshire)
3 fresh red or green chillies, skinned,
    seeds removed, cut into strips
hard-boiled egg slices for garnish

Cover the chicken with the stock and bring to the boil, skimming off any foam that forms. Reduce the heat and simmer until the chicken is tender but not falling off the bone. Remove the chicken, drain and cool. Remove the skin from the chicken and shred the meat into 5-cm/2-in long pieces.

Cover the breadcrumbs with half the milk and leave until the bread has absorbed the milk. Mash the bread to make a paste.

Sauté the onion and garlic in 2 tablespoons of the oil until soft. Add the chillies, walnuts, salt and pepper, and simmer for 5 minutes. Stir in the remaining oil and bread paste and stir until thoroughly mixed. Gradually add the remaining milk, stirring constantly, and heat until the sauce has thickened.

Add the chicken and cheese and simmer until the chicken has heated and the cheese has melted. Garnish with the chilli strips and egg slices.

Serve with boiled potatoes or rice.

Heat scale 3

Pepper Prawns

BRAZIL

Serves 6

Palm hearts add an authentic touch to this classic Brazilian dish. They are now available in cans in many supermarkets.

1 small onion, thinly sliced
1 clove garlic, finely chopped
1 red or green pepper, cut in matchstick strips
2 tbsp peanut oil
4 tsp crushed red chillies, or ¼ tsp cayenne
2 small tomatoes, peeled and chopped
3 tsp chopped fresh parsley
1 tsp dried basil
700g/1½ lb uncooked prawns, peeled and de-veined
25g/1 oz flour
3 tbsp butter
2 tsp cornflour, mixed with 2 tbsp water
1 can palm hearts, drained

Sauté the onion, garlic and pepper in the oil until soft. Add the crushed chillies, tomatoes, parsley and basil. Cover and simmer for 30 minutes.

Dredge the prawns in the flour, then sauté them in the butter until golden brown.

Stir the cornflour mixture into the sauce and heat until slightly thickened. Add the prawns and palm hearts and heat for 5 minutes.

Serve over rice, or accompanied by baked yams or sweet potatoes.

Heat scale 3

Fish Fillets in Coconut Milk

COLUMBIA

Serves 4

Coconuts are prevalent along the Caribbean coast of South America, so it's not surprising to see a fish dish with coconut milk in this region. Compare this one to recipes from Southeast Asia and the Pacific.

4 white fish fillets, each cut 2.5-cm/1-in thick
4 fresh green chillies, skinned, seeds removed, chopped
2 medium tomatoes, peeled and chopped
1 small onion, chopped
450ml/¾ pt coconut milk (page 87)
4 tbsp double cream

Place the fish in a pan and cover with the chillies, tomatoes, onion and coconut milk. Simmer for 10 minutes, or until the fish is opaque. Remove the fish and keep warm.

Continue to simmer the sauce until it is reduced to 250ml/8 fl oz. Strain the sauce, stir in the cream, and heat until warm. Pour over the fish and serve.

Heat scale 4

Vatapá de Camarao e Peixe

BRAZIL

Fish and shellfish in coconut-nut sauce is a classic Bahian dish that clearly illustrates the African influence in Brazil.

Serves 6

900g/2 lb uncooked prawns or shrimps, peeled and de-veined
900g/2 lb white fish fillets, cut in 5-cm/2-in pieces
4 tbsp oil
1 small onion, finely chopped
6 small hot green (serrano) chillies, finely chopped, or ¾ tsp cayenne
1 tsp ginger
1 tsp paprika
2 medium tomatoes, peeled and chopped
300ml/½ pt milk plus 2 tbsp extra
250ml/8 fl oz Coconut Milk (page 87)
50g/2 oz ground roasted peanuts
50g/2 oz ground cashew nuts
½ tsp coriander seeds
salt and pepper to taste
2 tbsp flour mixed with 2 tbsp cold water

Lightly brown the prawns or shrimps and the fish in the oil, adding the prawns or shrimps a few at a time. Remove and drain. Add the onion and sauté until soft and transparent. Reduce the heat and add the chillies, ginger, paprika and tomatoes. Cover and cook over medium heat for 10 minutes.

Stir in the milk, coconut milk, peanuts, cashews, coriander, salt and pepper and simmer over low heat for 15 minutes. Stir in the flour mixture and cook until slightly thickened, stirring constantly. Purée the sauce until smooth. Return the sauce to the pan and cook, stirring constantly, until thick. Add the fish and prawns or shrimps and simmer until thoroughly heated.

Serve with or over rice, accompanied by slices of fresh orange, papaya, banana, pineapple and mango, and a green vegetable.

Heat scale 4

Bolivian Baked Corn

Serves 4

Almost a soufflé, this corn casserole goes well with any grilled or roast meat. It also makes a delicious buffet or brunch dish.

1 tbsp flour
3 tsp crushed red chillies
15g/½ oz butter
450g/1 lb corn kernels, thawed if frozen
2 eggs, beaten
225g/8 oz Gruyère or Emmental cheese, grated

Sauté the flour and the chillies in the butter. Combine the corn and eggs and add to the chilli mixture, stirring well. Pour half the corn mixture into a greased casserole dish and cover with half the cheese. Add the remaining corn and top with the remaining cheese. Bake for 45 minutes to 1 hour at 180°C/350°F/Gas mark 4.

Columbian Hot Marrow, Chilli Cheese Potatoes, Vatapá de Camarao e Peixe

Chilli Cheese Potatoes

Heat scale 5

PERU

The marinated onions provide the pungency in this dish, which utilizes a food staple of the country, potatoes.

Serves 4–6

¼ tsp cayenne, or to taste
6 tbsp lemon juice
¼ tsp salt
1 large onion, sliced and separated into rings
225g/8 oz Cheddar cheese, grated
250ml/8 fl oz double cream
3 fresh green chillies, skinned, seeds removed, chopped
2 tbsp olive oil
6 potatoes, boiled and diced
1 fresh green chilli, skinned, seeds removed, cut in strips

Mix the cayenne, lemon juice and salt. Add the onion rings and toss until coated. Cover and marinate at room temperature for 30 minutes. Drain.

Combine the cheese, cream and chopped chillies in a blender or food processor and purée until smooth. Heat the oil and slowly add the cheese mixture, stirring constantly. Simmer over a low heat until the sauce thickens, about 5 to 10 minutes.

Serve the sauce poured over the hot potatoes. Garnish with the drained onion rings and the strips of chilli.

Columbian Hot Marrow

Heat scale 3

Serves 6

The presence of sugar in this vegetable casserole shows the influence of the Spanish – their preference for sweeter dishes. This one can be served as a side vegetable dish or for lunch. Originally made with vegetable squash, we have adapted this recipe for marrows or courgettes.

1 large onion, sliced and separated into rings
1 red or green pepper, sliced
25g/1 oz butter
4 fresh red chillies, skinned, seeds removed, finely chopped, or 4 dried red chillies that have been rehydrated by soaking in water to cover
3 tbsp flour
4 tbsp brown sugar
150 ml/¼pt water
4 tomatoes, peeled and quartered
salt to taste
½ a small marrow, or 450g/1 lb large courgettes, sliced
175g/6 oz Cheddar cheese, grated

Sauté the onion rings and pepper in the butter until soft. Add the chillies and flour and cook until the flour begins to brown. Gradually add the brown sugar, add the water and cook over a low heat for 5 minutes. Place the tomato quarters over the mixture, add salt to taste, and cook for an additional 10 minutes.

In a greased ovenproof casserole, alternate layers of the vegetable and the tomato mixture. Top with the grated cheese and bake at 160°C/325°F/Gas mark 3 for 35 to 40 minutes.

The Caribbean Islands

Because of the patterns of European colonization, the West Indies contain such a wide range of food styles that the food of the area can hardly be termed a cuisine. When Columbus landed in these islands, he did, indeed, 'discover' chillies as far as the Old World was concerned. He took back seeds that eventually spread the cultivation of *Capsicum annuum* around the world. On the isles of the Caribbean, however, the Indians were already cooking with them. The first settlers on these islands, the Arawaks and the Caribs, apparently brought chillies with them from South America and began cultivation. Then the Spanish, English, Dutch and French colonists brought their foods to the islands, and the African slaves added theirs. Quite a combination!

The most common hot ingredients used on the islands include green chillies and curries, which utilize the smaller hot chillies like serranos and jalapeños. Chillies are usually combined with poultry, seafood, goat meat, vegetables and rice. Curiously, ginger, which is grown extensively in Jamaica, is not found in many of the island recipes.

Heat scale 4

Spicy Chicken Soup

CURAÇAO

Serves 6–8

Here is a soup from the Dutch Antilles that verges on being a fully fledged stew. It is definitely a meal in itself.

1–1.5-kg/2–3-lb oven-ready chicken
2 l/3½ pt chicken stock
4–5 green chillies, skinned, seeds removed, chopped
2 potatoes, peeled and diced
100g/4 oz peas
2 yams, peeled and diced
3 tomatoes, peeled and chopped
100g/4 oz marrow or courgettes, diced
100g/4oz sweetcorn
1 medium onion, diced
salt and pepper to taste

Combine the chicken and stock in a large pan and bring to the boil. Reduce the heat, cover, and simmer for 1 hour, or until the chicken is cooked. Skim off any foam that surfaces. Remove the chicken, pull the meat from the bones and chop. Reserve the stock.

Allow the stock to cool in the refrigerator and remove the fat that rises to the surface. Return the chopped chicken to the pan, add the remaining ingredients, and bring to the boil. Reduce the heat and simmer until the vegetables are tender, about 30 minutes.

Heat scale 4

Jamaican Red Bean Soup

Serves 6

The combination of beans and soup is very common in the islands, and the soups are usually quite pungent. The red beans used are often called 'red peas' or Mexican chilli beans. If you use dried red kidney beans, be sure they boil rapidly for 10 minutes before simmering. This removes any harmful toxins. Canned beans only need heating through.

6 small hot green chillies (jalapeño or serrano), chopped, or 4 larger green chillies, chopped plus a few drops Tabasco sauce
275g/10 oz dried red kidney beans, washed and drained, or 2 large (439g/15 oz) cans red kidney beans
1 medium onion, chopped
2 stalks celery, chopped
100g/4 oz salt pork, chopped
1.4 l/2½ pt water

Combine all the ingredients in a large pan or slow-cooker. Bring to the boil, boil for 10 minutes, then reduce the heat and simmer for about 3 hours or until the beans are done. Add more water if necessary. If using canned beans, drain and add to the remaining ingredients, but cook just until the meat and vegetables are tender. Use Tabasco sauce for instant heat, as some of the chilli flavour may be lost.

Purée until smooth and strain. The soup should be thick. Reheat the soup before serving.

Heat scale 2

Jamaican Yam Crisps

Serves 8

Traditionally served as an hors d'oeuvre, yam crisps are an unusual delicacy.

4 yams
75g/3 oz brown sugar
⅛ tsp cayenne
100g/4 oz crushed plain digestive biscuits
100g/4 oz butter
2 tbsp oil

Bake the yams in their skins for 1 hour in an oven set at 180°C/350°F/Gas mark 4. Cool, peel, and cut into thin strips about 2.5 × 5 cm/1 × 2 in.

Combine the brown sugar, cayenne and crushed biscuits. Dip the yam strips in the mixture and toss until well coated. Fry the strips in hot butter and oil, turning often, until browned on all sides.

Chilli Seafood Salad, Jamaican Red Bean Soup, Chilli Veal

Heat scale 4

Fish in Escabeche

CUBA

Needs advance preparation

Serves 6–8

Escabeche is a Spanish word meaning 'pickled'. It also describes a dish popular in many Spanish-speaking countries where a fish is first cooked, then marinated in a spicy vinegar sauce. The longer you keep it, the more the flavours mellow.

900g/2 lb firm-fleshed white fish,
    cubed
3 tbsp olive oil
2 medium onions, sliced
2 cloves garlic, chopped
150ml/¼ pt red wine vinegar
4 dried red chillies, whole
¼ tsp dried thyme
¼ tsp dried marjoram
3 whole peppercorns

Fry the fish cubes in the oil until lightly browned, adding extra oil if necessary. Remove with a slotted spoon and drain.

Sauté the onion and garlic in the oil in the pan until soft. Place the fish in a glass or ceramic dish and top with the onions, garlic and oil.

Heat the wine vinegar with the remaining ingredients and simmer for 15 minutes.

Pour the vinegar marinade over the fish and chill in the refrigerator for at least 24 hours.

Serve garnished with sliced green olives as a starter, with crusty bread.

Heat scale 3

Chilli Sauce for Seafood

GUADELOUPE

Makes about 250ml/8 fl oz

There are an infinite number of island variations on sauces to accompany seafood or poultry. Lime juice and chillies are a combination common to most.

1 medium onion, finely chopped
juice of 2 limes
25g/1 oz butter
1 clove garlic, mashed or minced
2 small hot green chillies (jalapeño
    or serrano), finely chopped, or 2
    large green chillies, finely
    chopped plus 2 drops Tabasco
    sauce
salt to taste

Marinate the onion in the lime juice for 1 hour, then drain and reserve the marinade. Sauté the onion in the butter until soft. Add the garlic, chillies, lime marinade and salt. Cook over a low heat for 15 minutes and cool before serving.

Serve with grilled fish or chicken.

Haitian Pepper Sauce

Heat scale 7

Makes about 300ml/½ pt

This fiery sauce is traditionally served as an accompaniment to fish or poultry.

5–6 red or green hot chillies (jalapeño or serrano), finely chopped
100g/4 oz papaya, finely chopped
3 medium onions, finely chopped
3 cloves garlic, finely chopped
½ tsp turmeric
3 tbsp malt vinegar
1 tsp salt
a few drops Tabasco sauce (optional)

Combine all the ingredients in a saucepan and bring to the boil, stirring constantly. Reduce the heat and cook for an additional 5 minutes. Put the mixture in a blender or food processor and purée until smooth. Allow to cool to room temperature before serving. Adjust hotness with Tabasco sauce, if necessary.

Picadillo

Heat scale 4

Cuban Hash

Serves 4–6

There are variations of this dish in virtually every Spanish-speaking country in the Western Hemisphere, though many recipes are not as hot as this one. Once again, make it as hot – or as bland as you like.

900g/2 lb lean beef or pork, cut in 2.5-cm/1-in cubes
2 tbsp oil
2 onions, finely chopped
5–6 fresh green chillies, skinned, seeds removed, chopped
2 cloves garlic, finely chopped
3 red or green peppers, finely chopped
salt and pepper to taste
6 tomatoes, peeled and chopped
¼ tsp ground cloves
75g/3 oz raisins
6 stuffed green olives, sliced
¼ tsp ground cinnamon
2 tbsp red wine vinegar
75g/3 oz blanched almonds, chopped

Brown the meat in the hot oil. Add the onions, chillies, garlic, peppers, salt and pepper, and sauté for 5 minutes or until the vegetables are soft. Add all the remaining ingredients, except for the almonds, and simmer over low heat for 25 to 30 minutes or until the meat is tender. Sprinkle the almonds over the hash before serving.

Serve as a meal in itself, but Picadillo is also excellent with baked yams or sweet potatoes and rice.

Variation Add sliced bananas and chopped pineapple and cook for 15 minutes, then garnish with almonds.

Heat scale 2–3

Spiced Meat Loaf

ST CROIX

Serves 6–8

Ah, an exotic variation of an American favourite! Instead of serving with mashed potatoes, try baked plantains or yams.

900g/2 lb minced beef or pork
1 medium onion, chopped
1 egg, beaten
75g/3 oz breadcrumbs
salt and pepper to taste
4 tbsp Red Chilli Sauce (page 146),
*   or drops of Tabasco to taste*
2 tbsp dry mustard
250ml/8 fl oz water
125ml/4 fl oz tomato purée
2 tbsp vinegar
2 tbsp brown sugar
2 tbsp pineapple juice
4 pineapple rings

Combine the beef or pork with the onion, egg, breadcrumbs, salt, pepper and Chilli Sauce or Tabasco. Form the mixture into a loaf shape, transfer to a roasting tin and smooth the top.

Make a sauce of the mustard, water, tomato purée, vinegar, sugar and pineapple juice. Spread this sauce over the top of the loaf and arrange the pineapple rings on top.

Bake at 180°C/350°F/Gas mark 4 for 1½ hours, basting frequently with the juices.

Heat scale 4

Chilli Pot

TRINIDAD AND TOBAGO

Serves 6

This is a modern adaptation of the Trinidadian recipe that traditionally requires the addition of cassareep, an extract of cassava root.

1.5-kg/3-lb oven-ready chicken, cut
*   into portions*
750ml/1¼ pt water
salt to taste
450g/1 lb pork or best braising steak,
*   cut into 2.5-cm/1-in cubes*
4–5 fresh red or green chillies,
*   skinned, seeds removed, chopped*
1 large onion, coarsely chopped
3 tbsp brown sugar
7.5-cm/3-in cinnamon stick
6 whole cloves
¼ tsp dried thyme
1 tbsp vinegar

Cover the chicken with salted water and bring to the boil. Boil for 10 minutes, skimming off any foam as it forms. Reduce the heat and simmer for 1 hour. Remove from the heat and allow the stock to cool. Skim off any fat that rises to the surface. Remove the chicken from the bone and chop the meat.

Add all the rest of the ingredients except the vinegar to the stock and simmer for an additional 45 minutes to 1 hour, or until the meat is tender. Add the vinegar just before serving.

Serve with baked yams or sweet potatoes.

Spicy Chicken Soup, Spiced Meat Loaf

Ropa Vieja Cubana

Heat scale 3

Cuban 'Old Clothes'

Serves 6

Despite the odd name – an idiom for leftovers – this is an extremely popular dish both in Cuba and among Cubans living elsewhere. In some versions it is served with lots of hot chillies, in others it is much more bland. Adjust the pungency to your own taste.

1kg/2 lb braising steak
1 large onion, coarsely chopped
1 tsp salt
1 bay leaf
450ml/³⁄₄ pt water
3 tsp finely chopped hot chillies (jalapeño or serrano)
2 garlic cloves, finely chopped
2 red or green peppers, finely chopped
2 tbsp olive oil
4 large tomatoes, peeled and chopped
¹⁄₄ tsp cinnamon
¹⁄₂ tsp ground cloves
2 carrots, diced
strips of canned pimento for garnish

Simmer the steak, half the onion, the salt and the bay leaf in the water for 1½ hours, or until the meat is tender. Remove the steak, strain the liquid and reserve the stock. Cut the steak into strips about 5 × 7.5 cm/¼ × 3 in.

Sauté the remaining onion, the chillies, garlic and pepper in the olive oil until soft. Stir in the tomatoes, cinnamon, cloves and carrots. Cook until the vegetables begin to break down and the mixture is thick.

Add the meat to this sauce together with 250ml/8 fl oz of the reserved stock. Cook until the meat is thoroughly heated.

Serve with rice and garnish with pimento strips.

Chilli Veal

Heat scale 2

ST LUCIA

Serves 4

The African influence on Caribbean cooking is illustrated here with the combination of chillies and peanuts.

4 veal or lamb chops
4 tbsp peanut butter
1 tbsp oil
4 spring onions, sliced
2 cloves garlic, chopped
250ml/8 fl oz white wine
2 fresh red chillies, skinned, seeds removed, finely chopped

Cover the chops with the peanut butter and allow to stand for 1 hour. Fry the chops in the oil to brown and remove from the pan. Sauté the onions and garlic in the pan juices until the onions are soft. Add the wine, chillies and the chops and cook slowly for 20 minutes, stirring occasionally.

Heat scale 3

Calabaza Stew

PUERTO RICO

Serves 4–6

Served with fresh, crusty rolls or corn bread, this hearty stew combines several staples of the island: pork, yams and plantains.

900g/2 lb pork, cut in 2.5-cm/1-in
   cubes
900ml/1½ pt water
1 sweet potato, peeled and sliced
¼ small marrow, cubed (see method)
1 yam, peeled and sliced
2 medium onions, chopped
2 cloves garlic, chopped
1 red or green pepper, chopped
3–4 fresh green chillies, skinned,
   seeds removed, chopped
3 tbsp oil
2 medium tomatoes, peeled and
   chopped
2 courgettes, cubed
2 plantains or bananas, sliced
juice of 2 limes

Put the pork in the water and bring to the boil. Reduce the heat and simmer covered for 45 minutes. Add the sweet potato, marrow, and yam and simmer for an additional 15 minutes.

Sauté the onions, garlic, pepper and chillies in the oil until soft. Add the onion mixture to the meat. Add the tomatoes, courgettes and plantains or bananas, and continue to simmer until the vegetables are tender – about 15 to 20 minutes. Stir in the lime juice and serve.

Heat scale 4

Curried Cabrito

JAMAICA

Serves 6–8

This is a traditional celebration dish in Jamaica, *cabrito* being young goat meat. Some variations add coconut milk or substitute lamb for the goat. We suggest you do the latter . . .

40g/1½ oz butter
2 tbsp oil
1.5-kg/3 lb lean cabrito (young goat)
   or lamb, cut into 2.5-cm/1-in
   cubes
2 onions, finely chopped
4 small hot chillies (jalapeño or
   serrano), finely chopped
½ tsp allspice
2 tbsp Curry Powder (page 23)
salt and pepper to taste
250ml/8 fl oz chicken stock
1 bay leaf
2 tbsp lime juice

Heat a third of the butter in the oil and brown the meat cubes, turning often. Remove the browned meat and keep warm.

Add the remaining butter and sauté the onions until soft. Add the chillies, allspice, curry powder, salt and pepper, and cook for 5 minutes over a low heat, stirring constantly.

Add the browned meat, stock and bay leaf and simmer for 1½ hours, or until the meat is tender. Remove the bay leaf, stir in the lime juice, and serve.

Serve the meat over rice with the sauce from the pan poured over the top. Garnish with slices of fresh papaya and mango.

Arroz con Pollo

Heat scale 5

DOMINICAN REPUBLIC

Needs advance preparation

Serves 4–6

This rice and chicken recipe is found everywhere in the Caribbean, although, of course, it varies somewhat from country to country. This particular recipe is interesting because the chicken is marinated first in a hot chilli sauce from the adjoining country on the same island.

6 tbsp Haitian Pepper Sauce (page 131)
1-kg/2-lb oven-ready chicken, cut into portions
4 tbsp oil
225g/8 oz rice
450ml/³⁄₄ pt chicken stock
1 red or green pepper, chopped
100g/4 oz peas
3 tbsp chopped canned pimentos

Pour the Pepper Sauce over the chicken and leave to stand at room temperature for 2 hours. Remove the chicken and reserve the marinade.

Heat the oil and fry the chicken pieces until lightly browned. Remove the chicken. Add the rice and sauté until lightly browned. Stir in the remaining ingredients, including the marinade. Add the chicken, cover and cook over a low heat until the rice is done and the chicken is tender, about 30 minutes.

Cuban Lobster Créole

Heat scale 5

Serves 4–6

This hot dish is excellent served with saffron rice and garnished with parsley. Use cooked crab or scampi instead of lobster, or substitute any firm-fleshed white fish.

900g/2 lb cooked lobster meat, diced
3 small hot chillies, finely chopped
4 tbsp oil
300ml/¹⁄₂ pt white wine plus 2 tbsp extra
double quantity Chilli Sauce for Seafood (page 130)
¹⁄₂ tsp dried oregano
chopped parsley for garnish

Sauté the lobster and chillies in the hot oil for 5 minutes, stirring constantly. Remove the lobster. Pour off all but 2 teaspoons of the oil and add the wine. Bring to the boil, reduce the heat and add the Seafood Sauce and oregano. Simmer the mixture for 3 minutes. Return the lobster to the pan and cook for 10 minutes, basting frequently. Garnish with parsley before serving.

Jamaican Yam Crisps, Arroz con Pollo

Heat scale 3

Peppered Crabs

DOMINICAN REPUBLIC

Crabs are frequently served on the islands by stuffing the empty shells with dishes such as this.

Serves 4

6 small hot green chillies, finely
    chopped
½ red or green pepper, finely
    chopped
4 medium onions, finely chopped
2 cloves garlic, finely chopped or
    crushed
2 tbsp oil
2 tomatoes, peeled and chopped
6 tbsp dry sherry
3 tbsp tomato paste
salt and pepper to taste
450g/1 lb cooked crab meat
125ml/4 fl oz lime juice
chopped parsley for garnish

Sauté the chillies, pepper, onions and garlic in the oil until soft. Add the tomatoes, sherry, tomato paste, salt and pepper and bring to the boil. Stir the mixture constantly and cook until most of the liquid has evaporated and the sauce begins to hold its shape.

Add the crab and stir into the sauce until it is well coated. Reduce the heat, cover and simmer until the crab is thoroughly heated. Pour the lime juice over the crab and garnish with the parsley.

Variation Substitute cooked white fish for the crab meat.

Heat scale 7

Prawns in Spicy Sauce

ST VINCENT

Lobster or scallops may be substituted for prawns in this fiery seafood dish.

Serves 4–6

8 small hot chillies, seeds removed,
    finely chopped
2 medium onions, finely chopped
2 stalks celery, finely chopped
2 tbsp oil
4 tomatoes, peeled and chopped
1 bay leaf
1 tbsp parsley, finely chopped
1 tsp sugar
salt and pepper to taste
900g/2 lb uncooked prawns, peeled
    and de-veined
a few drops Tabasco sauce
    (optional)
grated Parmesan cheese for garnish

Sauté the chillies, onions and celery in oil until the onions are soft. Add the tomatoes, bay leaf, parsley, sugar, salt and pepper. Cook until most of the liquid has evaporated and the sauce is quite thick. Reduce the heat, add the prawns or other seafood, cover and simmer for about 10 minutes, being careful not to overcook. Adjust 'heat' with Tabasco.

Serve over rice, and garnish with Parmesan cheese.

Chilli Seafood Salad

BAHAMAS

Needs advance preparation

Serves 4

In this recipe we are using an acid to 'cook' the raw fish. It is important to use either a glass or ceramic bowl – a metal container will produce a metallic taste.

4 small hot green chillies (serrano or jalapeño), finely chopped
½ tsp freshly ground black pepper
8–10 scallops, sliced
50g/2 oz canned pimento, drained and chopped
2 tomatoes, peeled and finely chopped
2 cloves garlic, crushed
1 medium onion, finely chopped
2 stalks celery, finely chopped
6 tbsp lime juice
3 tbsp oil
¼ tsp dried oregano
salt to taste

Combine all the ingredients and toss gently until the seafood is well coated. Marinate the mixture in the refrigerator for at least 6 hours or until the fish becomes opaque.

Variations Substitute scampi for the scallops, or use 225g/8 oz of any firm-fleshed white fish such as cod or haddock.

Salt Fish and Ackee

Jamaica's 'National Dish'

Needs advance preparation

Serves 4

Ackee is a firm, nutlike substance found inside the fruit of the ackee tree. Oddly enough, other parts of the same fruit are poisonous. It is so prevalent on the island that it is called 'free food'. Ackee is sometimes found canned in delicatessen shops, but if you can't find it, try this substitution: scramble 6 eggs in a nonstick pan without fat until firm.

450g/1 lb salt cod
1 medium onion, finely chopped
3 small hot chillies, seeds removed, finely chopped, or ¼–½ tsp cayenne
2 tbsp oil
¼ tsp dried thyme
225g/8 oz ackee or scrambled eggs (see above)

Soak the cod in cold water to cover for 24 hours, changing the water 4 or 5 times to remove excess salt.

Place the cod in a saucepan with just enough fresh water to cover it and simmer until the fish begins to flake. Drain and flake the fish, discarding bones, fins and other inedible parts. Set the flaked fish aside.

Sauté the onion and chillies or cayenne in the oil until the onion is browned, taking care not to allow it to burn. Add the fish, thyme and ackee or scrambled eggs and cook over a low heat, stirring often, until thoroughly heated.

Serve for breakfast or lunch with fresh fruit and rice.

The American Sunbelt

The term 'Sunbelt' here refers to the southern and south-western states of the United States, which were the areas originally influenced by the hot cuisines of other areas. The hot chilli sauces served with corn dishes in Texas, New Mexico, Arizona and California originated in the Mexican state of Chihuahua. Now considered suitable by international gourmets, such 'Mexican' food was originally peasant fare, as were many of the recipes that follow.

Because of the regional adaptations of chilli sauces and other 'hot' ingredients used in the Sunbelt, the term 'Mexican' cooking is no longer accurate. Cooking in California is far milder than in New Mexico, while Texans prefer the jalapeños to green chillies and Arizona chilli dishes tend to be sweeter than those from other states. The pungency of the chillies used varies enormously, and experimentation and tasting are the only ways to ensure that you do not burn your guests.

A collision of cultures in Louisiana and adjacent states produced a hot cuisine that looks to Tabascos and cayenne chillies for its heat. The French colonists (Créoles), French-Canadians (Cajuns), and freed African slaves all contributed to dishes in which the fiery element is usually added in the form of sauces and condiments after the food is cooked. Chillies are used in sauces for seafood, and cayenne is added as others would use salt and pepper. Since heat can be added to any food after cooking, we have included only those Créole and Cajun recipes in which hot ingredients are used during cooking.

And finally, we have added a few innovative recipes, such as Turkey with Chilli Stuffing, to show that with a little imagination you can 'heat up' a favourite traditional recipe of your own.

Heat scale 3

Pungent Vegetable Soup

NEW MEXICO

Serves 4–6

What a surprise this would be for your lunch guests! Perhaps it would be kind to warn them before serving this soup. It may be rather different from what they expect . . .

Spanish Spinach, Créole Jambalaya, Cream Cheese Chilli Dip

1 small onion, finely diced
2 medium carrots, finely diced
1 stalk celery, finely diced
40g/1½ oz butter
2 medium potatoes, diced
75g/3 oz whole corn kernels
4 tomatoes, peeled and chopped
1 l/1¾ pt chicken stock
1 tbsp chopped parsley
salt and pepper
4 tsp crushed dried red chillies

Sauté the onion, carrot and celery in the butter for 10 minutes. Add the potatoes and sauté for 10 more minutes. Add the rest of the ingredients and bring to the boil. Lower the heat immediately and simmer for 45 minutes to 1 hour, or until the vegetables are cooked and the soup is thick.

Heat scale 4

Cream Cheese Chilli Dip

NEW MEXICO

Needs advance preparation

Makes 250ml/8 fl oz

Although called a 'dip', this cream creese spread can be used as a stuffing for celery stalks, or spread on toast or crackers to make canapés.

3 green chillies, skinned, seeds
    removed, finely chopped
225g/8 oz cream cheese
2 tbsp milk
1 tbsp very finely chopped onion
pinch of garlic salt

Combine all the ingredients and beat until creamy, adding a little more milk if necessary. Allow the dip to sit for 1 hour or more before serving for the flavours to blend.

Serve as a snack with potato crisps, cheese biscuits or raw vegetables (*crudités*).

Heat scale 5

Salsa Fria

NEW MEXICO

Needs advance preparation

Makes up to 450ml/¾ pt

Salsa Fria or 'Cold Sauce' because it isn't cooked, is an all-purpose sauce that can be put on the table for general use. Although most commonly served with crisps as an appetizer, Salsa Fria can be used as an accompaniment to beef tacos or other Mexican foods. The keys to success with this sauce are *fresh* coriander and *very finely chopped* ingredients. Adjust the degree of heat by the number and type of chillies used. Fresh or canned green chillies may be used. This salsa is modelled on the recipe served at the La Florida Bar in Juarez, Mexico.

4–6 small hot green (jalapeño or
  serrano) chillies, very finely
  chopped
2 large onions, very finely chopped
2 large ripe tomatoes, peeled and
  very finely chopped
3 cloves garlic, very finely chopped
2 small bunches fresh coriander,
  finely chopped
3 tbsp red wine vinegar
3 tbsp oil
¼ tsp dried oregano
½ tsp salt (optional)

Mix all the ingredients together in a bowl and chill for at least 1 hour before serving.

Serve with crisps or tortilla chips. This sauce makes a perfect dip for an hors d'oeuvre before a huge Mexican-style dinner.

Heat scale 4

Chile con Queso

New Mexican Chillies and Cheese

Makes 600–750ml/1–1¼ pt

This makes an excellent party dip and any left over can be used as a hot cheese sauce with baked potatoes or other vegetables.

1 onion, finely chopped
3 tbsp oil
2 tbsp flour
450ml/¾ pt milk
3 tbsp water
2 tomatoes, skinned and chopped
4–5 fresh green chillies, skinned,
  seeds removed, chopped
450g/1 lb Cheddar cheese, grated

Sauté the onion in the oil until soft. Stir in the flour and heat for 2 minutes, stirring.

Combine the milk and the water and stir into the flour mixture, then heat until slightly thickened, stirring all the time. Add the tomatoes, chillies and the cheese. Stir over moderate heat until the cheese has melted.

Serve warm with crisps or tortilla chips, pouring the sauce into small warm bowls.

Heat scale 3

Louisiana Créole Cocktail Sauce

Needs advance preparation

Makes about 300ml/½ pt

In Louisiana this spicy sauce is a favourite one to serve with both prawns and oysters.

2–3 tbsp grated fresh horseradish
2 tsp Tabasco sauce
175ml/6 fl oz tomato ketchup
juice of ½ lemon or lime
salt to taste

Combine all the ingredients and purée until smooth. Let this mixture chill for at least 1 hour to blend all the ingredients.

Serve in cocktail glasses with large shelled prawns arranged over the rims, and a dish of lemon wedges. Garnish the sauce with 1 finely chopped hard-boiled egg.

Chilli Salad Dressing

Heat scale 3

NEW MEXICO

Makes up to 600ml/1 pt

This is New Mexico's answer to the famous American 'Green Goddess' dressing.

2–3 fresh green chillies, skinned,
   seeds removed, finely chopped, or
   3 small hot green (serrano) chillies,
   finely chopped
1 clove garlic, very finely chopped
1 medium onion, chopped
3 tbsp water
3 medium avocados, mashed
juice of 2 lemons or limes
pinch each of dried oregano, basil
   and thyme
175ml/6 fl oz salad oil

Purée the chillies, garlic and onion in the water. Add the mashed avocado, lemon or lime juice and seasonings and mix well. Gradually add the oil until the desired consistency is reached.

Serve with any crisp green salad, but this sauce is especially good with sliced tomatoes and garnished with parsley or fresh coriander.

Variation Add up to 6 tablespoons soured cream for a creamier dressing.

Barbecue Sauce

Heat scale 6

NEW MEXICO

Needs advance preparation

Makes about 450ml/³⁄4 pt

Chilli and mustard are combined in this 'biting' sauce. Spicy barbecue sauce first originated in the American South with Tabasco being added to a tomato-based sauce – but this one is definitely a South-western invention.

4 dried red chillies, crumbled
250ml/8 fl oz hot water
1 medium onion, chopped
1 clove garlic, very finely chopped
1 tbsp bacon dripping
¹⁄2 tsp cayenne or a few drops
   Tabasco sauce
3 tbsp bottled barbecue sauce
1 tsp dry mustard
6 tbsp tomato ketchup
2¹⁄2 tbsp vinegar
2 tbsp brown sugar
1 tsp Worcestershire sauce

Soak the chillies in the hot water for 15 minutes. Sauté the onion and garlic in the dripping until soft. Add all the remaining ingredients, and cover and simmer for 2 hours. Purée the mixture in a blender until smooth.

Serve with chicken, beef or pork. It is especially good for basting grilled and barbecued meats.

Variation For a milder sauce, leave out the cayenne.

Potatoes with Red Chilli, Green Chilli Stew, Chiles Rellenos

Red Chilli Sauce

Heat scale 5

NEW MEXICO

Makes up to 450ml/¾ pt

Make this basic sauce from fresh, 'pickled', or dried red chillies, or, if you prefer, use chilli powder. (Do not make it with cayenne if you value your life!) Remove the skins and seeds of the fresh red chillies before using. Remove the seeds and stems from dried pods. Dried Mexican pods such as chile negro or ancho may be substituted, if you can find them.

5 dried red chilli pods or the equivalent
250ml/8 fl oz water
2 cloves garlic, chopped
2 tbsp oil
1 medium onion, chopped
½ tsp ground cumin
½ tsp ground coriander
salt to taste

Tear the chilli pods into strips and soak them in hot water for 20 minutes. Purée the chilli and water in a blender or food processor until smooth. Add all the remaining ingredients and simmer for 1 hour. Remove the coarse sauce from the heat and blend it again to make a smooth sauce.

Serve with enchiladas, tacos, tamales, as a dip, or to accompany meat and poultry dishes.

Variation Add ¼ teaspoon cayenne for extra heat . . .

Salsa de Chile Verde

Heat scale 6

Basic Green Chilli Sauce

Makes about 450ml/¾ pt

Most of the cooked chilli sauces served are made with dried red chilli pods. This green sauce is more commonly found in the American South-west, particularly in New Mexico, where the recipe originated.

1 large onion, chopped
2 cloves garlic, finely chopped
2 tbsp oil
5–6 fresh green chillies, skinned, seeds removed, chopped
1 large tomato, peeled and chopped (optional)
½ tsp ground cumin (optional)
½ tsp ground coriander (optional)
350ml/12 fl oz water
salt to taste

Sauté the onion and garlic in the oil until transparent, add the remaining ingredients, and simmer for 30 minutes.

Serve this versatile sauce with enchiladas, tacos, tostados, as a dip, or to accompany beef, chicken or fish.

Variations Purée in a blender for a smoother sauce. Omit the tomato for a 'purist's' sauce. Add 1 or 2 ground dried chillies for a hotter sauce.

Chile con Carne

Heat scale 6

TEXAS

Serves 6

There are probably a million recipes for this immensely popular dish, and half a dozen cookbooks specializing in its variations. Although purists may feel the addition of beans is an adulteration, we advise you to follow your own preferences.

900g/2 lb braising steak, cut into
   1-cm/½-in cubes or minced
2 tbsp oil
1 large onion, chopped
1 clove garlic, chopped
7 dried red chillies, seeds removed,
   crumbled
750ml/1¼ pt water
3 tomatoes, peeled and chopped
   (optional)
½ tsp dried oregano
¼ tsp dried basil
¼ tsp cumin (optional)
salt to taste
350g/12 oz cooked kidney or pinto
   (borlotti) beans (optional)

Brown the meat in the oil, add the onion and garlic, and sauté until the onion is soft.

Blend the chillies in a third of the water. Add the chilli mixture and the remaining water to the meat and simmer for 1 hour. Add all the other ingredients, except the beans, and simmer for 1 hour more. Add more water if necessary. Add the beans and cook until the mixture is thick, about 15 to 30 minutes.

Serve with corn bread and coleslaw.

Red Chile con Carne

Heat scale 7

NEW MEXICO

Serves 6–8

This is a New Mexican version of the dish, which means beans are *never* used. It is easy to prepare and the flavour of the chilli improves if prepared a day in advance.

750ml/1¼ pt water
6–8 dried red chillies
900g/2 lb pork, cut into 2.5-cm/
   1-in cubes
2 tbsp oil
3 cloves garlic
salt to taste

Heat a third of the water to boiling, then pour it over the chillies and let them steep for 15 minutes.

Fry the pork in the oil until lightly browned. Pour off the excess fat.

Purée the chillies and garlic in the steeping water until smooth. Add the chilli mixture and the remaining water to the pork. Bring to the boil, then reduce the heat and simmer until the pork is very tender and starts to fall apart, at least 2 hours.

Heat scale 6

Fajitas

TEXAS

Needs advance preparation

Serves 8

Texans love to barbecue and are quite inventive when it comes to outdoor cooking; try the following recipe.

4 tbsp jalapeño juice (from canned jalapeños)
4 tbsp soy sauce
4 tbsp port wine
900g/2 lb grilling steak
8 flour tortillas (page 111)
4 tbsp canned jalapeños, or other canned hot peppers, finely chopped
Salsa Borracha (page 98)

Combine the jalapeño juice, soy sauce and port. Trim and score the meat and marinate in the sauce for 24 hours.

Grill the steak over charcoal or under a hot grill until done, and carve diagonally against the grain in thin strips.

Place pieces of steak in a flour tortilla, cover with the chopped jalapeños and eat like a sandwich, dipping into the Salsa Borracha.

Heat scale 6

Chile Verde con Carne

Green Chilli Stew

Serves 6

This is another of New Mexico's staple dishes – no cold winter Sunday would be complete without a football game and a bowl of green chilli. There are many variations of this dish, so experiment with your own.

900g/2 lb braising meat (pork preferred, or use beef), cut into 2.5-cm/1-in cubes
2 tbsp oil
2 large onions, chopped
1 clove garlic, chopped
1 l/1¾ pt water
6–8 green chillies (or more for heat), skinned, seeds removed, chopped
2 large tomatoes, peeled and chopped
2 large potatoes, chopped (optional)
¼ tsp cumin (optional)
salt to taste

Brown the meat in the oil, add the onions and garlic, and sauté for 10 minutes. Put the water in a casserole or a slow-cooker with all the other ingredients. Add the meat, onions and garlic, and cook for 2 or more hours or until the meat is very tender and starts to fall apart.

Serve as a main dish, or as the basis of a number of other recipes (see below).

Variations An old El Paso favourite is *Caldillo*, a dish very similar to the above except that braising steak is used. Potatoes are common in *Caldillo* and occasionally jalapeños (the small hot green chillies) are substituted for the larger fresh green chillies. Left-over chilli stew can be turned into a delicious casserole by lining a baking dish with risen bread dough or pastry, pouring in the stew, and topping it with grated Cheddar cheese. Bake for 45 minutes at 180°C/350°F/Gas mark 4.

Dave's Barbecued Chilli-Cheese Steak

Heat scale 5

Serves 4

4 tsp lemon juice
2 large thick frying steaks, sirloin or
   fillet preferred
2–4 garlic cloves, finely chopped
2 tsp freshly ground black pepper
6–7 fresh green chillies, very finely
   chopped
100g/4 oz Cheddar cheese, grated

The addition of chillies and cheese creates perhaps the perfect steak of all time – according to one of us at any rate!

Sprinkle the lemon juice over each side of the steaks. Then sprinkle each side with the garlic and black pepper, and pound them gently into the meat. Leave the steaks to sit at room temperature for at least 1 hour.

Barbecue the steaks over hot coals or grill them indoors. About 6 minutes before the meat is done, if barbecued, 3 minutes if grilled, sprinkle first the chillies, then the cheese over the steaks and cook until the cheese on top has just melted.

Serve, halved, with a baked potato and a crisp green salad.

Créole Jambalaya

Heat scale 4

LOUISIANA

Serves 6–8

Most recipes for this dish play down the hot ingredients, but our informants in Louisiana insist that Tabasco and cayenne are essential in this Spanish-Créole favourite. And the Créoles are known for seasoning liberally with cayenne!

40g/1½ oz butter
450g/1 lb pork, cut into 1-cm/½-in
   cubes
2 large onions, minced
100g/4 oz cooked ham, cut into 1-
   cm/½-in cubes
5 cloves garlic, very finely chopped
1 tsp thyme
2 bay leaves
1 tbsp finely chopped fresh parsley
½ tsp ground cloves
225g/8 oz Italian sausage or salami
750ml/1¼ pt hot beef stock
350g/12 oz long-grain rice
¼ tsp cayenne
2 tsp Tabasco sauce

Melt the butter in a saucepan and add the pork and onion. Sauté until the onion is soft and the pork is lightly browned. Add the ham, garlic, thyme, bay leaves, parsley and cloves and sauté for an additional 5 minutes.

Coarsely chop the sausage, add to the pork mixture, and sauté for 5 minutes. Then add the stock and bring to the boil. Reduce the heat and simmer for 10 minutes.

Add the rice, cayenne and Tabasco and bring back to the boil, then reduce the heat and cook for about 20 minutes, stirring occasionally, until the rice is cooked and the stock has been absorbed.

Serve as a meal on its own, or turn it into a feast with a green salad and French bread.

Texan-style Pork Ribs

Serves 6–8

Ginger and small hot Mexican chillies called pequíns are behind the pungency of the original recipe for these sweet-and-sour ribs. However, pequíns are not generally available, so use cayenne or Tabasco instead. These ribs can be cooked outdoors on a barbecue or grilled indoors.

2kg/4½ lb pork spare ribs in a rack
4 cloves garlic, whole
1 tsp cornflour mixed with 1 tbsp
  water
250ml/8 fl oz pineapple juice
2 tbsp soy sauce
2 tbsp vinegar
1 tsp ground cumin
¾ tsp cayenne, or more to taste, or
  1 tsp Tabasco sauce
2 tsp very finely chopped fresh ginger
10 pineapple rings (fresh preferred)

Rub the ribs vigorously with the garlic and set aside.

Combine the cornflour mixture, pineapple juice, soy sauce, vinegar, cumin, cayenne or Tabasco, and ginger in a pan. Slowly bring to the boil, reduce the heat, and simmer until the sauce is thick, stirring constantly.

Place the ribs on a barbecue or under a grill. Baste the exposed side with the sauce, and baste again in 5 minutes. After 10 minutes, turn the ribs and baste the second side and cook 10 minutes more.

If you are using a grill, place the pineapple rings on the ribs and baste both the rings and ribs with the sauce and cook for about 15 minutes more.

If you are cooking over coals, turn the ribs a second time, place the pineapple rings on top and baste a final time. Cook for about 10 minutes more.

Serve with roasted corn on the cob and potato salad.

Carne Adovada

NEW MEXICO

Needs advance preparation

Serves 6

This recipe has been prepared in New Mexico for hundreds of years. Before the advent of refrigeration, it was a convenient way of preserving pork, as the chilli acts as an antioxidant to retard deterioration. Traditional Carne Adovada is extremely hot.

750ml/1¼ pt water
225g/8 oz dried red chilli, coarsely
  crumbled
4 cloves garlic, very finely chopped
900g/2 lb pork, cut in 5-cm/2-in
  strips

Pour about 6 tablespoons hot water over the chillies and leave to stand for 20 minutes. Put the chillies, garlic and remaining water in a blender and purée. Cover the pork strips with the chilli sauce and marinate for 24 hours in the refrigerator.

Bake the pork in the marinade for 3 hours in an oven set at 150°C/300°F/Gas mark 2.

Serve Carne Adovada like a stew in a shallow bowl accompanied by flour tortillas.

Posole

Heat scale 6

NEW MEXICO

Serves 6

Christmas in New Mexico would not be the same without a bowl of the traditional posole, though this dish is also popular throughout the year. There are many variations of posole – this is the best we can do out of New Mexico. It is an easy-to-prepare 'stew' that can be cooked in a slow-cooker. Posole is a lime-dried corn, unlikely to be available, so use canned hominy or whole corn kernels.

450g/1 lb canned hominy, or fresh or
*   frozen corn kernels*
6 tbsp chilli powder
900g/2 lb lean pork, diced
1 onion, chopped
2 cloves garlic, very finely chopped
2 tsp dried oregano (optional)
1 tsp vinegar
salt to taste

Cover the hominy with water and simmer until the kernels 'pop'. If using corn, bring it to the boil.

Add the remaining ingredients and return to the boil. Reduce the heat, cover and simmer until the pork is very tender and begins to fall apart. Add more water if necessary.

Chicken Chimichangas

Heat scale 4

ARIZONA

Serves 4

Here is a very popular dish from Arizona. How and where it originated is a mystery; the word 'chimichangas' has no English translation – it may as well be called 'thingummyjig'. Basically, a chimichanga is a deep-fried burrito, or filled tortilla.

2 medium onions, chopped
25g/1 oz butter
13–14 green chillies, skinned, seeds
*   removed, chopped*
225g/8 oz cooked chicken, shredded
6 tbsp soured cream
50g/2 oz Cheddar cheese, grated
50g/2 oz black olives, chopped
4 large flour tortillas (page 111)

Sauté the onion in butter until soft, then combine all the ingredients for the filling. Divide the filling between the tortillas, placing equal amounts in the middle of each. Fold up the top and bottom and sides. Secure with wooden toothpicks if necessary. Deep-fry in hot oil, turning constantly, until browned all over.

Serve each Chimichanga covered with Guacamole (page 99) or soured cream, and with Refried Beans (page 108) and rice.

Variations Almost any type of filling can be used. Substitute beef, pork or Refried Beans for the chicken. Green Chilli Stew or Red Chile con Carne can also be used.

Tamale Pie with Chicken and Cheese

Heat scale 4

NEW MEXICO

By varying the accompaniments, this casserole can be served for lunch or as a hearty dinner. It has the basic tamale characteristics but is much easier to prepare.

Serves 6–8

The filling
2-kg/4-lb oven-ready chicken
2 large onions, sliced and separated
 into rings
2 cloves garlic, very thinly sliced
1 tsp dried basil, crushed
2 whole cloves
1 bay leaf
4 green chillies, skinned, seeds
 removed, chopped
1/4 tsp cayenne or 2 cayenne chillies
1 tsp chilli powder
100g/4 oz ripe olives, chopped
175g/6 oz corn kernels, thawed if
 frozen
450ml/3/4 pt soured cream
salt to taste

The topping
450 ml/3/4 pt chicken stock from
 recipe
100g/4 oz *masa harina* (fine maize
 flour, *not* corn meal)
2 eggs, separated
225g/8 oz Cheddar cheese, grated

Simmer the chicken with half the onion, the garlic, basil, cloves and bay leaf in water to cover until the chicken starts to fall away from the bone. Remove the chicken and strain and reserve the stock.

Remove the meat from the bone and chop the chicken and remaining onion. Combine with the remaining ingredients, except the reserved stock. Place in a casserole dish and cover with the topping.

For the topping, bring the stock to the boil and gradually add the maize flour (*masa harina*) while stirring constantly. Reduce the heat and cook until the mixture thickens, about 10 minutes. Remove from the heat and stir in the egg yolks. Whip the egg whites until stiff and fold them into the *masa* (maize flour) mixture. Spread this topping over the casserole and sprinkle thickly with the grated cheese.

Bake for 35 minutes at 190°C/375°F/Gas mark 5.

Serve with an avocado and grapefruit salad, or with a green vegetable such as peas, green beans or courgettes.

Ginger-fried Southern-style Chicken

Heat scale 1

A traditional favourite, cleverly disguised.

Serves 4

100g/4 oz flour
6 tsp ground ginger
4 chicken breasts
a little milk (see method)
salt and pepper

Mix together the flour and most of the ginger. Dip the chicken in the milk and let the pieces drain. Lightly sprinkle the chicken with the rest of the ginger, salt and pepper, then coat the chicken with the seasoned flour.

75g/3 oz butter
150ml/¼ pt oil

Brown the chicken pieces quickly in the hot butter and oil. Cover the pan and cook for 20 minutes. Remove the lid and cook until the chicken is brown and tender, about 20 minutes more.

Serve with a cream gravy, mashed potatoes and green beans.

Turkey with Chilli Stuffing

Heat scale 3

Serves 6–8

By adding chillies to a traditional Christmas turkey, you will certainly add to the warmth of the occasion.

100g/4 oz butter
1 large onion, chopped
6–7 fresh green chillies, chopped
2 stalks celery, chopped
450–550g/1–1¼ lb wholemeal
    breadcrumbs
100g/4 oz pine nuts or chopped
    walnuts
2 tsp dried thyme
about 300ml/½ pt chicken stock
4.5–5.5kg/10–12 lb oven-ready
    turkey

Melt the butter in a saucepan and fry the onion until soft. Combine the onion, chillies, celery, breadcrumbs, nuts and thyme in a bowl and mix thoroughly. Add enough stock to moisten thoroughly, but not saturate the mixture.

Stuff the cavity of the turkey and sew or skewer closed. Roast the bird at 180°C/350°F/Gas mark 4 for 25 minutes per 450g/lb, basting the bird every 15 minutes or so with the pan juices, and with a little extra melted butter if necessary.

Serve with roast or mashed potatoes, gravy and vegetables.

Chiles Rellenos

Heat scale 3

NEW MEXICO

Serves 4

Here is a classic dish: stuffed whole chillies. Properly prepared, they are incredibly delicate. However, if you find these too hot to handle, use peppers instead.

8 whole green chillies, fresh or
    canned, skinned, seeds removed
Cheddar cheese, cut into sticks
4 eggs, separated
4 tbsp flour
2 tsp baking powder
1 tbsp water
¼ tsp salt
flour for dredging
oil for deep-frying

Cut a slit in each chilli and stuff with cheese sticks. Pat dry and set aside.

Beat the egg whites until stiff. Combine the remaining ingredients, including egg yolks, and gently fold in the egg whites to make a batter.

Roll the stuffed chillies in flour and carefully dip them into the batter and coat well. Deep-fry the chillies, turning them constantly until lightly browned. Remove and drain.

Serve topped with a chilli sauce (either red or green) and the traditional accompaniments, rice and beans.

Variations Chillies can be stuffed with a variety of fillings including Picadillo (page 131) or minced meat plus cheese. For a Chiles Rellenos casserole, line a baking dish with the stuffed chillies, pour the batter over the top, and bake for 40 minutes in a 180°C/350°F/Gas mark 4 oven. Pour your choice of sauce over the top before serving.

Heat scale 5

Chilli and Spring Onion Pie

ARIZONA

This sunny 'quiche' makes an excellent lunch dish.

Serves 6–8

The pastry
175g/6 oz plain flour
½ tsp salt
1 tsp grated lemon rind
100g/4 oz butter
4 tbsp chilled white tequila or vodka

The filling
4 tbsp melted butter
2 tbsp dried breadcrumbs
75g/3 oz Parmesan cheese, grated
2 spring onions, chopped (including green parts)
4 eggs
2 egg yolks
1 tsp dry English mustard
1 tsp Dijon mustard
salt to taste
¼ tsp cayenne
600ml/1 pt milk, scalded
3–4 green chillies, skinned, seeds removed, chopped
1 tbsp white tequila or vodka
a dash of chilli powder

For the pastry case, sift the flour and salt and add the lemon rind. Cut the butter into pieces and, using your fingertips, rub it into the flour mixture until it looks like coarse breadcrumbs. Use the chilled tequila or vodka to work the dough until it holds together.

On a lightly floured surface, roll out the dough until it is large enough to fit a 25-cm/10-in diameter flan tin. Place the dough in the tin and shape it to fit firmly and trim off the excess dough. Line the crust with buttered aluminium foil and hold it in place with dried beans, rice or rock salt.

Bake in a 180°C/350°F/Gas mark 4 oven for 15 minutes. Remove the foil and beans, and prick the pastry base all over with a fork. Return the pastry case to the oven and bake, uncovered, for an additional 10 to 15 minutes or until golden brown.

Place the cooked pastry case on a baking sheet and brush the bottom of the pastry with 1 tablespoon of the melted butter. Combine the breadcrumbs with 2 tablespoons of the Parmesan cheese and sprinkle the mixture over the bottom of the pastry case.

Sauté the spring onions in 2 tablespoons of the melted butter until soft, then set aside.

Combine the eggs and egg yolks and whisk until thick. Stir in the two mustards, salt and cayenne and blend well. Stir the remaining cooled melted butter into the mixture. Mix all but two tablespoons of the Parmesan cheese into the scalded milk and stir into the egg mixture. Add the green chillies, tequila or vodka and cooked spring onions. Mix well and pour into the pastry case.

Bake at 180°C/350°F/Gas mark 4 for 30–40 minutes or until the filling sets. Remove from the oven, top with the remaining Parmesan cheese, sprinkle with the chilli powder, and serve.

New Mexico Pizza Special

Needs advance preparation

Serves 2–4

Innocently resembling a normal pizza, this seemingly innocuous dish will get immediate attention with the first bite.

1 package pizza dough or bread mix

The sauce
1 large onion, chopped
2 cloves garlic, crushed
2 tbsp oil
175ml/6 fl oz tomato paste
4 tbsp tomato ketchup
1 tbspdried oregano or marjoram
1 tsp sugar
salt and pepper

The topping
3–4 fresh green chillies, cut in strips
3 medium onions, chopped
50g/2 oz mushrooms, sliced
50g/2 oz black olives, sliced
1 sweet Italian sausage, crumbled
50g/2 oz grated mozzarella cheese
50g/2 oz grated Provolone or
  Cheddar cheese
50g/2 oz grated Parmesan cheese
a little olive oil

Make up the pizza or bread dough as instructed on the package and leave to rise. Meanwhile, make the sauce.

Sauté the onion and garlic in the oil until soft. Add the remaining ingredients, bring to the boil, then lower the heat and simmer until thick – up to 2 hours. Remove and purée in a blender or food processor until smooth.

Punch down and spread the pizza or bread dough to fit a 25-cm/10-in pizza pan or shallow ovenproof plate. Spread the sauce over the dough and arrange the topping – the chillies, onions, mushrooms, olives and sausage – on top of the sauce. Sprinkle with the grated cheeses and then sprinkle with a little olive oil.

Bake at 200°C/400°F/Gas mark 6 for about 25 minutes, or until the crust is lightly browned.

Potatoes with Red Chilli

NEW MEXICO

These are South-western hash brown potatoes with a 'bite'.

Serves 4

3 tbsp oil or bacon dripping
salt to taste
2 large or 4 medium potatoes, diced
1 small onion, diced
1 tbsp red chilli powder

Heat the oil or dripping and several pinches of salt in a frying pan, then add the potatoes and fry until tender. Remove the potatoes, add the onion and chilli powder to the oil, and sauté. Add the potatoes and fry until the potatoes are well browned.

Serve with Huevos Rancheros (page 106). They add colour and heat to a grilled steak served with peas or corn.

Heat scale 4

Courgettes with Corn and Green Chilli

CALIFORNIA

Serves 6

The staples of pre-Columbian America are combined in this vegetable casserole.

175g/6 oz corn kernels, drained and dried
2 tbsp oil
2 onions, chopped
1 clove garlic, very finely chopped
4–5 green chillies, skinned, seeds removed, chopped
4 large courgettes or small marrows, diced into cubes
salt and pepper to taste

Fry the corn in the oil for 5 minutes, stirring constantly so it does not burn. Add the onions, garlic and chillies and cook until the onions are soft. Add the remaining ingredients and cook over a low heat until the courgettes are tender.

Serve with roast or grilled meat.

Variation To make a casserole, put the cooked vegetable mixture in a dish, add 250ml/8 fl oz milk mixed with 2 tablespoons flour, and top with grated cheese. Bake for 20 minutes at 160°C/325°F/Gas mark 3.

Heat scale 4

Green Rice

NEW MEXICO

Serves 6

Here is a New World pilaf variation that is very versatile and simple to prepare. It probably originated in Mexico after rice became a staple there and was later introduced into the American South-western states.

225g/8 oz long-grain white rice
2 tbsp butter or oil
1 onion, finely chopped
4 green chillies, skinned, seeds removed, chopped
2 cloves garlic, very finely chopped
1 l/1¾ pt chicken or beef stock

Sauté the rice in the butter or oil until golden brown. Add the onion and sauté until soft, about 5 minutes. Take care not to let the rice burn.

Purée the chillies, garlic and a little stock until smooth. Add this to the rice and continue cooking over a low heat for 5 minutes. Stir in the remaining stock and transfer this mixture to a baking dish. Cover and bake at 180°C/350°F/Gas mark 4 for 45 minutes. Fluff with a fork before serving.

Serve with poultry, fish and red meat dishes. Simply vary the type of stock used.

Variations Substitute red chillies for the green and you have . . . red rice. Uncover the dish for the final 15 minutes of baking for crisper rice.

Spanish Spinach

Heat scale 3

NEW MEXICO

Serves 4

Two favourites, chillies and pinto (borlotti) beans, are combined with spinach in this traditional New Mexican dish.

3 tbsp chopped onion
2 cloves garlic, very finely chopped
2 tbsp bacon dripping
1 tbsp dried chilli seeds or dried red chilli pods, crushed
450g/1 lb spinach, cooked and drained
100g/4 oz pinto (borlotti) beans, cooked
1 tsp vinegar
salt

Sauté the onions and garlic in the bacon dripping until soft. Add the remaining ingredients and fry for 10 to 15 minutes.

Chilli Corn Bread

Heat scale ?

Serves 6

A quick and easy spicy bread that goes very well with soups and stews.

298g/10½ oz can creamed corn
350g/12 oz cornmeal
75g/3 oz margarine or butter, melted
2 eggs, slightly beaten
3–4 tbsp milk
1 tsp baking powder
½ tsp baking soda
1 tsp sugar (optional)
1 tsp salt
175g/6 oz Cheddar cheese, grated
3 green chillies, skinned, seeds removed, chopped

Combine all the ingredients except the chillies and cheese. Pour half the mixture into a greased 23×23 cm/9×9 in baking pan. Sprinkle half the cheese and chillies on top. Add the remaining batter and top with the rest of the cheese and chillies. Bake in a 200°C/400°F/Gas mark 6 oven for 45 minutes. Cool slightly before serving.

Index